D1569015

Terrorism, Politics and Law

WITHDRAWN FROM
CANISIUS COLLEGE LIBRARY

WITHDRAWN FROM
CANISIUS COLLEGE LIBRARY

19.95

Terrorism, Politics and Law.

The *Achille Lauro* Affair

ANTONIO CASSESE

Princeton University Press

Princeton, New Jersey

HV
6431
.C3813
1989

Copyright © Antonio Cassese 1989

Published by Princeton University Press,
41 William Street, Princeton, New Jersey 08540

All rights reserved

Library of Congress Cataloging-in-Publication Data

Cassese, Antonio.
    Terrorism, politics, and law: the Achille Lauro affair. / Antonio
Cassese
    p.   cm.
    Bibliography: p.
    Includes index.
    ISBN 0–691–07838–6:
    1. Terrorism.   2. Achille Lauro Hijacking Incident, 1985.
    3. Italy—Politics and government—1976–   I. Title.
HV6431.C3813 1989
364.1′552′0945—dc19   89–3971
                                                                CIP

CANISIUS COLLEGE LIBRARY
BUFFALO, N. Y.

Printed in Great Britain

Contents

Foreword

Not everyone has heard of Emmerich de Vattel, the great Swiss jurist who, in 1758, published a book entitled *The law of nations or principles of the law of nature applied to the conduct and affairs of nations and sovereigns*. So modern were its concepts and so limpid its style that for over a century the book became a bible for diplomats and politicians, as well as for jurists, judges and military men. Vattel tried to introduce a note of moderation and rationality into international affairs in an era in which – as Hegel pointed out in 1810 – relations among states were more 'natural' than 'legal', because 'natural bodies [states] are violent in their mutual behaviour: they see to it that their own rights are respected, enforcing this respect by themselves, and, therefore, they end by waging war on one another.' Vattel, on the other hand, had studied the 'natural principles' of the behaviour of states in order to pinpoint such rules of conduct as might curb the high-handed power of princes. To a large extent he was successful, thanks also to the incisiveness of his ideas and the clarity with which he laid them before his readers (rare qualities even then, when erudite and indigestible treatises were held in high esteem, especially in the academic world).

At a certain point in his book Vattel made the following observation: 'International law is the law of sovereigns. It is written mainly for them, and for their ministers. In truth, it should interest all men and, in a free Nation, its precepts should be the study of all its citizens. But it would be of little

use to individuals who are not called upon to run states and
who do not determine their actions in any way.' Doubtless,
these remarks were valid in the eighteenth century, when
international relations were almost exclusively in the hands of
princes and their ministers; it was up to the foreign ministries
to determine alliances, to decide when to make war or peace,
to see to the protection of nationals abroad, to define the
means and limits of colonial expansion, and so on. However,
his words no longer apply to the world we live in. Although, to
a large extent, international affairs are in the hands of
governments, private pressure groups and public opinion, at
home and abroad, can sway their decisions. In addition, at
least some classes of peoples, as well as intergovernmental
organizations, can now use the various international forums to
speak to states. International law is no longer a tool handled
exclusively by national governments; it can also be used by
individuals, by private organizations and by certain categories
of peoples. An international lawyer should no longer write for
rulers alone (who may or may not heed his words); he ought
now to write mainly for ordinary citizens: he should offer
them parameters by which to judge international affairs, and
analytical mechanisms for examining the intricacies of the
world community. As ordinary citizens we can easily lose our
bearings, because it is so difficult to comprehend the world in
which we live, unless we *know the facts* (so often left unsaid or
filtered and distorted by the media) and are furnished with
conceptual guidelines.

That is the reason why I decided to write this book. I have
tried to delve into a pernicious phenomenon currently
besetting the world community: terrorism. I thought that the
best approach to this complex problem did not lie in
canvassing all the relevant international facts and legal
instruments. Rather, after briefly surveying the basic approach
taken by the world community towards terrorism, I deemed fit
to make a searching analysis of one significant episode in our
recent history – the hijacking of the *Achille Lauro* – in order to
see whether one could pluck the facts from such a tangle and

thus evaluate the behaviour of the governments involved. The *Achille Lauro* affair strikes me as emblematic. It is an episode from which it is possible to extract the marrow and which can, therefore, help us understand certain symptomatic features of international affairs today.

I have written this book for the layperson, whom Vattel, on the whole, decided to ignore. It is his interest that must be aroused if one wishes to reduce violence in international relations to a tolerable level; that is, if one hopes to hamper the use of force, to eradicate terrorism and diminish the crushing effects of oppressive government, both in interstate relations and in those between states and individuals, one must not neglect the role of ordinary citizens. Jurists who deal with international law, like their colleagues who study municipal law, would do well to remember what Hitler said, at a time when his desire to dominate the world had not yet made him lose all contact with reality: that a day would come, in Germany, when it would be considered a 'disgrace' to be a jurist. This would come about when the machinery of state and the whole structure of international relations were transformed into a perfect bureaucratic mechanism; then all those whose job it is to create, interpret and modify legal standards, as well as to criticize those that already exist, would become redundant. There would no longer be any need for people who challenge the way in which those standards are applied; nor for people who insist that whoever transgresses those standards should be made to answer for their actions. I strongly believe that, in reacting to these aberrations, one should make an effort to act as a 'jurist' and try to comprehend and evaluate why 'others' behave in a given way: when such behaviour is unlawful one ought to 'contest' it before the appropriate court, whether international or municipal, or pillory it before the 'jury' of public opinion. Nowadays, the latter is regarded with diffidence because it is so easily manipulated, both by overt and hidden means. I believe (at least, I hope) that the 'jurists' of whom Hitler spoke so disparagingly can help at least a section of that public opinion to put aside their prejudices and judge world events.

This book developed initially out of a lecture I gave at the Catholic University of Louvain in November 1986, as the holder of the 'Chaire Henry Rolin' for that year. The ensuing discussion, and particularly the remarks made by Professor Salmon and Professor Rigaux, was most useful. I have also taken advantage of observations and critical comments that two 'actors' in the *Achille Lauro* affair (Mr Giuliano Amato, at that time Under-Secretary of State attached to the Prime Minister, Bettino Craxi; and Mr Antonio Badini, then diplomatic adviser to the Prime Minister) were so kind as to make, in a personal capacity, after reading the first draft of the book. Other distinguished friends and colleagues (Roberto Barsotti, Tullio Padovani and Paolo Tonini) also helped me with their criticisms and suggestions.

The Italian version of this book was first published by Editori Riuniti in 1987, under the title *Il caso 'Achille Lauro'*. This English edition, while based on a translation of the Italian text, is, to a large extent, a completely new book. I have deleted a number of sections dealing with Italian domestic practice which I thought might be of less interest to non-Italian readers. I have also revised my views on various matters concerning compliance during the affair with the 1983 United States–Italy extradition treaty. Finally, I have added new material on terrorism generally. In this regard I was greatly assisted by the lively discussion at a conference on terrorism in April 1988 (at which I had an opportunity to present a paper on the subject of terrorism and the international community), held at Ditchley Park, Oxfordshire, England and organized by the Institute for Study of Terrorism in conjunction with University College, London. I also had a very useful, informal exchange of ideas on the *Achille Lauro* affair with Judge A. Sofaer, Legal Adviser to the US Secretary of State, at that same conference.

I should like particularly to thank Jennifer Greenleaves, who carried out the translation of the Italian text with her usual skill and sensitivity and Andrew Clapham who reviewed the translation from a legal perspective. I am greatly indebted also to Susan Marks, who assisted me in preparing this revised edition of the book with great perceptiveness and legal acumen.

Finally, I should like to thank all those who, with kindness and forebearance, satisfied my insatiable appetite for unpublished or untraceable documents. I am especially grateful to the Genoa Judges (Lino Monteverde, President at the Appellate Court of Assizes; Judge Enzo Giacalone and also the President of the Juvenile Court), as well as Miss Lucia Fiore, who worked at the office of the diplomatic adviser to the Prime Minister. Naturally, any errors or misunderstandings still contained in the text are entirely my own responsibility.

1

The International Community and Terrorism

Terrorism can hardly be called a new phenomenon on the international scene. It is well-known that both the practice and the word itself were born during the years of the Jacobin terror (1793–4). Whatever its origin, in the nineteenth century it was widespread in many states (when the murder of monarchs and statesmen was fairly frequent), and in our own time it has become endemic to the international community. Today terrorism is a nightmare haunting that community, along with the threat of nuclear conflict, the chasm yawning between industrialized countries and underdeveloped ones, the ever more frequent cases of 'conventional' armed conflict within and between states, and the increasing occurrence of glaring violations of human rights.

If, within this general framework, one takes a look at the incidence of terrorism by *non-state* groups, these fall into four separate patterns. The first type is of *highly ideological inspiration*. This may be Marxist, in the broadest sense of the term (e.g. the terrorist groups in Western Europe in such countries as France, Italy and the Federal Republic of Germany), or religious (think, for example, of Islamic fundamentalism, which uses terrorism as one of its forms of action and penetration abroad). Although these two 'variants' are both based on a strong 'ideological' impulse – that is, on motives that are not mainly economic or political – they have little in common and their political and social roots are profoundly different.

A second form seems to be inspired by *ideals of national independence*. Take, for example, the IRA in Northern Ireland, the Basques, the Kurds, the Tamils, and so on. In each case one ethnic group is struggling to free itself from another 'dominant' group and to acquire independent status within the international community. One should point out that the governments opposed by these groups are not necessarily authoritarian or oppressive; in some cases they are prepared to grant some measure of automony to the ethnic group in question. The latter, however, not content with a limited sphere of action, continues to struggle for complete independence, and uses terrorism as one means for achieving this goal.

A similar form of terrorism is that used by certain national liberation movements, fighting in the name of the *principle of the self-determination of peoples*. Take, for example, movements such as the African National Congress in South Africa, the South West African People's Organization (SWAPO) in Namibia, the Palestine Liberation Organization (PLO), and the various groups in Eritrea that are fighting against the central government of Ethiopia. As in the second form, the group using terrorism is ethnically different from the ruling group and is also struggling for independence. The difference, however, lies in the fact that here the group – being subject to colonial or alien domination – falls squarely within the accepted, United Nations definition of 'peoples' having the right of self-determination. The very existence of this principle lends such groups an autonomous identity; it makes it easier for the international community to recognize and accept them than groups of the second type, which fall outside the terms of the United Nations definition.

Armed bands and movements that are fighting *oppressive regimes* are essentially different; these are of the same ethnic, religious and racial background as the governments they oppose. Think, for example, of the various movements, which often resort to terrorism, that are fighting, or have fought, against military dictatorships in Latin America.

Can we add yet another form of terrorism to that of the four private, or non-state, types I have listed: terrorism protected, encouraged or even organized by states? Some western governments think that Libya and Iran, at least, have given and still give financial and logistic support to terrorist groups that attack foreign countries. Of course, it is not easy to find concrete proof of the connection. Yet, at least in one case (the capture and detention of US diplomats as hostages by Iran in 1980), the International Court of Justice held that Iran, as an international subject, had kept the American diplomatic and consular staff prisoners. Although, at first, that state was merely responsible for omitting to arrest the 'students' who had captured and detained the Americans, later on it became more deeply involved: the hostages' gaolers acted as the official agents of Iran. Thus, in certain circumstances, some states have certainly been found guilty of acts of terrorism, just like non-state armed groups that also use terrorism.

Naturally, it is very hard to identify the *causes* of the current expansion of terrorism. Let me just mention a few circumstances that have given an impetus to or, to a certain extent, encouraged the phenomenon. One contributing factor is certainly the existence of harshly authoritarian structures within many states, not to mention profound social and economic inequalities among states. Yet another factor is the progressive fragmentation of the various centres of power in the international community, and the corresponding proliferation of poles of interest. The international community is no longer crystallized into a few great blocs, dominated by one great power, well able to control any centrifugal tendency. Since the two superpowers, which together could dominate the world, find it difficult to reach agreement, the international community has now split into many centres of power of varying size, each with a modicum of authority; these centres tend to protect and aid private groups in other state communities, because they share common ideological, political and religious roots.

Another important factor is the inability of the international community in its organized forms (especially the United Nations) to offer an adequate 'response' to requests for greater international justice, and to the need for preventive mechanisms to defuse economic and social conflicts both at a national and transnational level. A further factor is the spread of utopian ideologies, as well as doctrines of human rights. These give rise to or strengthen groups that are – to a greater or lesser degree – oppressed and encourage them to feel it is legitimate to fight for their freedom, independence and self-determination. As such groups almost invariably lack the means to fight in a 'conventional' way, they begin to conduct their battle by way of terrorism.

It might, therefore, be argued that the international community itself endorses, and sometimes legitimizes, some of the aspirations that underlie terrorism, even though the means used to assert these aspirations are condemned with great firmness by the majority of states, as I shall now show.

THE INTERNATIONAL COMMUNITY'S RESPONSE

The exposure of terrorism

Let us now inquire how the institutions of the world community have responded to terrorism: have they endorsed it, or have they condemned it? If the latter is true, was the condemnation unanimous and absolute, or was it evasive and qualified? Further, what effective legal tools have been introduced as a response to terrorism, at an institutional level?

Judge A. D. Sofaer wrote in 1986 that any evaluation of states' efforts to suppress or repress the phenomenon of terrorism was bound to reach a 'painful conclusion':

The law applicable to terrorism is not merely flawed, it is perverse. The rules and declarations seemingly designed to curb terrorism have regularly included provisions that demonstrate the absence of international agreement on the propriety of regulating terrorist activity. On some issues, the law leaves political violence unregulated. On other issues the law is ambivalent, providing a basis for conflicting arguments as to its purposes. At its worst the law has, in important ways, actually served to legitimize international terror, and to protect terrorists from punishment as criminals. These deficiences are not the product of negligence or mistake. They are intentional.

Should one agree with such a pessimistic view? However well-founded Sofaer's assessment, I disagree on various scores.

First, he does not recognize that important progress has been made as regards the definition of terrorism. Admittedly, there is not yet complete consensus on what constitutes terrorism, but there are at least the beginnings of a convergence of views on this subject. From the 109 different definitions identified by the American political scientist, Walter Laqueur, a much smaller number of common elements are beginning to emerge.

A number of states have, in municipal legislation, formulated definitions of terrorism. The United Kingdom Prevention of Terrorism (Temporary Provisions) Act 1984, for example, provides in Section 14(1) that 'terrorism means the use of violence for political ends and includes any use of violence for the purpose of putting the public or any section of the public in fear.' However, such broad definitions – which at their widest extent would include even resort to war – are of limited utility in the international sphere. A more precise definition is needed if we are to reach a situation where those who commit acts of terrorism can no longer claim to legitimize their acts by, in effect, 'defining them away'.

Useful elements for such a definition can already be found in the various treaties concluded between states on this subject, together with the resolutions of such international bodies as the UN General Assembly and international conventions on wars between states, and between states and national liberation movements. Various points may be deduced from this voluminous legal material; any *violent* act against *innocent people* intended to force a state, or any other international subject, to pursue a line of conduct it would not otherwise follow is an act of terrorism. Such acts are prohibited both in times of *peace* and in cases of *armed conflict*, whether civil strife, a war of national liberation or an armed conflict between states.

Obviously, when these acts involve attacks not on civilians but on the military, on the police and other state bodies of the same kind, the issue is far more difficult. Here, we must turn to the rules defining the conditions under which a fighter who is not a member of a state's regular armed forces may be considered a legitimate combatant and not a terrorist or other kind of criminal. In my view the Geneva Protocol I of 1977 (Additional to the 1949 Geneva Conventions) reflects the current customary international law on this matter. The Protocol provides, in essence, that, to qualify as a legitimate combatant, the fighter must *carry arms openly* for a certain period before the military operation, as well as during the operation; this will serve to distinguish him from civilians in the same area. Further, like any other combatant, he must respect the laws governing the conduct of hostilities and those relating to prisoners of war. Thus a commando attack on a military objective is to be considered belligerent action and not an act of terrorism, so long as the members of the commando carried their arms openly, as I have just said. On the other hand, holding a soldier or a policeman hostage, so as to obtain certain 'concessions' from the state to which the hostage belongs is always to be considered a form of terrorism, because it is contrary to international law – both that applying in peace time and that applying during war.

Secondly, the international community has made progress in its *basic attitude* to terrorism. Great strides were made between 1972 (the first year in which the UN General Assembly adopted a resolution on terrorism, after the massacres at Lod airport in Israel, and at the Olympic Games in Munich) and 1985 (when the UN Security Council and General Assembly adopted by *consensus* – in fact, unanimously – a number of important resolutions condemning terrorism). More recently, in 1987, a further resolution condemning terrorism was adopted by the UN General Assembly, though this time with opposing votes from the United States and Israel. These opposing votes were not, however, motivated by any reluctance to condemn terrorism. Rather, the United States and Israel were opposed only to that part of the resolution which proposed the convening of a conference to agree on a definition of terrorism; their fear was that a definition might emerge that distinguished terrorism as something intrinsically different from the activities of national liberation movements. In this regard it is clear that many Third World states, with the support of countries of the socialist bloc, have long taken the view that it is quite legitimate for those fighting for self-determination to use all available means to achieve their ends. Their most recent statements on the matter are still somewhat ambiguous. In 1985, for instance, the Angolan representative in the General Assembly, stated that 'acts of terrorism cannot be compared, under any pretext, with the acts of those who are fighting colonial and racist oppression, and for their freedom and independence.' Similar statements were also made by the delegates of Algeria, Bulgaria, Kuwait and Sri Lanka. More recently, in 1986, the PLO representative at the Security Council stated: 'the acts of violence by freedom-fighters against their oppressors and against the alien forces of occupation should never be confused with acts of terrorism.'

One interpretation of these statements is that the activities of national liberation movements *per se* cannot be equated with terrorism; in other words, just because these movements are comprised of irregular combatants fighting against governments, this does not mean they should be seen by the international community as criminal organizations. Certainly this proposition seems to me correct. However, the prevailing interpretation of these statements in Western countries is this view to which I have just referred, that the ends of self-determination are justified by any means, no matter how inhumane.

Means for combating terrorism

Let us now examine the ways in which the international community has, in effect, responded to terrorist attacks: what means have been devised to try to prevent or put an end to such attacks?

Our task will be made easier if we first distinguish between two possible forms of response: the one *peaceful*, the other *violent* (that is involving the use of force). In the first class we may place all those international treaties (whether bi- or multilateral) drawn up to concert the anti-terrorist efforts of states. As we shall see later, these treaties are usually aimed at specific forms of terrorism (the taking of hostages, the hijacking of aircraft, etc.) and they provide for close international cooperation as to the capture and imprisonment of the criminals, as well as laying down rules for their trial or extradition. The other response consists in the use of armed force to repress acts of terrorism, that is, to put an end to crimes of this kind (by destroying terrorist bases and killing the terrorists), or prevent their recurrence.

A review of the various international rules in this area reveals three important facts.

First, as it now stands, the international community insists that a choice should be made between the two possible responses: only after every effort has been made to solve the problem by peaceful means are states allowed to turn to military options as *extrema ratio*.

Secondly, given the current deficiencies of international enforcement mechanisms, *in practice* states either do not or cannot conform to the international community's 'command' to use the 'peaceful response' first. In other words, states often feel constrained to 'cut corners' and respond with armed force. Further, in some cases, for reasons that may be ideological, political or military, they may *prefer* such a response, opting for it *at once*, while the international community does no more than issue a purely verbal condemnation of their action.

Thirdly, the laws on the two possible 'responses' are of differing kinds: rules concerning a 'military response' are part of general (i.e. customary) international law and possess all the limits that are characteristic of this category, as well as the advantage that they are binding on all subjects of international law. On the other hand, the provisions for a peaceful response are part of treaty law: as such they are clearer and more precise (within certain limits that I shall describe later on), but they have one basic flaw, typical of treaty law: they are binding only on those states that have ratified or acceded to the relevant treaty (that is, those states that have agreed to be bound by the treaty provisions).

At this juncture it may prove useful to take a quick look at the contents of these two 'responses' to international terrorism.

The peaceful response, as I have already said, is based on multilateral and bilateral treaties. To date it has not been possible to draft a universal convention on the entire phenomenon of terrorism (the 1937 Convention, approved by the League of Nations, was a total failure since it was signed by only twenty-four states and ratified by one, India). Only one regional agreement has been reached so far on terrorism taken as a whole (the 1977 European Convention on the Suppression of Terrorism). On the other hand, there have been multilateral treaties on single aspects of terrorism: the hijacking of aircraft (the 1970 Hague Convention); the sabotage of aircraft (the 1971 Montreal Convention); terrorist attacks on 'internationally protected persons', that is, heads of state and heads of government, foreign ministers, diplomats, etc. (the 1973 New York Convention); the taking of hostages (the 1979 New York Convention). To these we should add the various international conventions on the humanitarian law of armed conflict, that are intended, among other things, to ban the use of terrorism during wars between states, wars of national liberation and civil wars (the four 1949 Geneva

Conventions and the two 1977 Additional Geneva Protocols). The latest legal instrument on this matter, the 1988 Convention for the Suppression of Unlawful Acts against the Safety of Maritime Navigation, was drafted as a direct result of the *Achille Lauro* incident. I shall revert to it in chapter 8.

In addition to these multilateral agreements, states have frequently used bilateral treaties, which usually cover extradition, as well as cooperation between judiciaries. Though they are not specifically concerned with terrorism, they can be used – and often are used – for acts of terrorism, if both contracting states are involved (for example, if a terrorist carries out an act of terrorism in the territory of one state, or against its citizens and its possessions, and then takes refuge in the territory of the other state; or when two states decide to cooperate to find and arrest a terrorist, or to extradite him to a third state – naturally, if the requisite conditions are fulfilled). In the *Achille Lauro* case, as we shall see in a later chapter, the provisions of a bilateral treaty became extremely relevant.

The main aim of all these treaties is to organize the prevention and especially the repression of terrorism by *individual contracting states*, each one within the limits imposed by its domestic legal system. In other words the parties to these treaties seek to *coordinate* the national coercive and judicial measures they adopt so as to be able to suppress terrorism and bring terrorists to justice in their own territory, or cooperate with another state that is doing so. In short, far from ruling out coercion against terrorists, these treaties lay down rules for the use of force against terrorists. However, force is used only by a state's own agencies acting within its own boundaries.

In many ways these international legal instruments are important and effective. For instance, all the multilateral treaties I have just quoted accept the principle *aut judicare aut dedere*: the contracting state on whose territory the author, or alleged author, of a terrorist crime is found, must either try him or hand him over to the other contracting party that requests his extradition according to the treaty provisions. In other words, these treaties provide for *universal jurisdiction*: any contracting state has the power and duty to try a terrorist who has sought refuge on its territory, even if he is not a national of that state and has not injured its possessions or harmed its citizens.

What, however, are the main shortcomings of these treaties? In my opinion there are three. First, the fact that not enough states have agreed to be bound by these conventions (as I have said, treaties are binding only on those states that have ratified them, thereby accepting their provisions) is an extremely difficult obstacle to overcome. Secondly, these conventions are severely hampered by the fact that they make no provision for effective enforcement mechanisms in case of violation. Should a party not respect the treaty provisions, other parties can do no more than apply the traditional (peaceful) sanctions authorized by the international community, which notoriously fail to yield satisfactory results. Thirdly, except for the 1977 European Convention on Terrorism, these treaties normally do not specify that terrorist crimes cannot be regarded as 'political offences' and as such exempt from extradition. This lacuna or ambiguity can lead to misunderstandings and misapplication of the treaty rules. It will continue to so do until it is universally accepted that terrorist crimes, though usually inspired by political motives, are so contrary to the accepted rules of intercourse among states as not to be entitled to the 'advantages' states generally accord to political offences.

Obviously, diplomats and jurists still have to work long hours, for many years, before they will be able to hammer out more satisfactory legal instruments.

Let us now turn to the international rules on 'armed response' to terrorism – in other words, the use of force by a state in the territory of another state or in areas not subject to territorial sovereignty (the high seas, international airspace). Before we examine these rules, it is worth emphasizing that terrorist groups, which operate on a vast scale in more than one state, would find it hard to survive without some degree of support from state apparatuses. Except in rare cases, this means that terrorist groups can usually count on the support and aid of a state (or even several states). Such backing may take various forms, according to the degree to which the state is involved. At one end of the scale, individuals may commit acts of terrorism abroad as legal or *de facto* state agencies: this is 'state terrorism'. Secondly, a state may choose not to act via its own agencies, but employ 'unofficial agents' or 'mercenaries': that is, armed bands that are organized, equipped, commanded and controlled by the state. Thirdly, a state may merely provide financial aid or weapons to the terrorists. In the fourth case the state provides logistic support, for example by training terrorists within its national territory. Fifthly, a state may not back the terrorists in any active manner (by providing aid, arms, etc.) but may consent to their seeking refuge in its territory; the latter becomes a convenient 'sanctuary' for terrorists before and after performing acts of terrorism against foreign countries. Finally, apart from these cases in which a state gives a terrorist group backing or help in other forms, a group not receiving any help from any country may carry out attacks on vessels on the high seas or on planes in international airspace.

In each of the hypotheses I have just listed, can a state that has been directly damaged by acts of terrorism react with force against the state which provided support to the terrorists, and if so, to what extent? As is well-known (and as will be discussed at greater length in chapter 5) the only justification for individual states resorting to force is 'the inherent right of individual or collective self-defence if an armed attack occurs...' (Article 51 of the UN Charter). Thus, it will be an essential condition for a forcible response to terrorism that the state itself was the victim of terrorist activity amounting to an 'armed attack' (individual self-defence) or that the state had been requested or previously authorized to assist another state which was the victim of such terrorist activity (collective self-defence). It will be a further essential condition that the state against which force is used can, in law, properly be held responsible for the terrorist activity amounting to an 'armed attack'. This said, we can go on to see what kind of response is authorized by international law in the various instances.

Let us first deal with the first and second hypotheses (terrorism by state agencies or armed bands controlled by a state). The state is authorized to use force by the general principle of self-defence against an 'armed attack' by another state, carried out (whether officially or unofficially) by that state's agencies. The 'armed attack' may take the form of very serious attacks against the territory of the 'injured' state, or of attacks against its agencies or citizens. It may also be in the form of terrorist actions against its citizens when they are abroad: in another country, on the high seas or in international or a third state's airspace. All that is required by international law is that the 'armed attack' be not merely sporadic or isolated, but part of a whole pattern of terrorist action. Further, international law requires the reaction to be 'proportional' to the attack and to be preceded by attempts at finding a peaceful solution. Even in the third form (when states provide the terrorists with arms or financial aid) the legal regulation provided by international law is clear. Numerous states now give arms and money to terrorists without this being considered by other states so unlawful as to be treated as the equivalent of an 'armed attack' legitimizing a military 'response'. One may therefore deduce that this type of aid, though banned by international law, can only warrant peaceful sanctions. International law is quite clear, too, as to the sixth situation (when a state is not involved in any way in terrorist actions on the high seas or in international airspace). In such a case, the state to which the ship or aeroplane belongs may use force against the terrorists. In addition, in this case, as in the first and second hypotheses, international law allows for 'collective self-defence', within the limits I mentioned earlier.

By contrast, international rules on the other two forms of states' possible involvement in terrorist action (aid in the form of 'logistic support', or the concession of 'sanctuary' to terrorists) are uncertain and ambiguous. Here both international practice and the legal literature are vacillating and contradictory. The matter was recently addressed by the International Court of Justice in the *Nicaragua v United States* case. The Court there held that, although the provision to rebels of logistical support, financial aid and weapons violates international law (especially the fundamental principle of non-interference in the domestic affairs of another state), such assistance is not normally sufficient to involve the assisting state in an 'armed attack'. Accordingly, it cannot justify resort to force in self-defence (whether individual or collective). Judges Jennings and Schwebel, by contrast, took the view that the provision to insurgents of logistical support, or at least logistical support coupled with weapons, will generally be sufficient to render the assisting state responsible for an 'armed attack' carried out by the insurgents. A number of influential commentators have also taken this view.

In the end this is clearly an area where it is difficult to formulate generalized rules. As both Judge Jennings and Judge Schwebel indicated, logistical support may take many forms. At one end of the scale it may involve the entire training, moving, lodging and equipping of an insurgent army, assistance which should, in my view, engage the state's responsiblity for attacks by the troops; at the other end of the scale it may involve merely permitting insurgents to sleep in disused huts in remote border areas, assistance which, in my view, should not of itself engage the state's responsibility for an armed attack. However, as is commonly the case, the area between the two extremes remains 'grey'.

Just as much uncertainty surrounds the other form of state involvement (when a state allows terrorists to use its territory as 'sanctuary'). Whereas there is ample agreement that in such a case the state is violating international law, some construe this behaviour as tantamount to 'armed attacks' justifying self-defence. This view has been advanced by South Africa and Israel within the Security Council, as well as in the writings of Professor Dinstein. Others, however, hold that in such cases the violation can be countered only by peaceful sanctions. Yet again the situation has not been regulated by clear and precise rules because states themselves disagree on what form these rules should take.

Before turning to other matters, I should like to add just one point. It is pleasing to note that at least the condemnation of terrorism (and the acceptance of the use of force as legitimate against terrorists in the cases I have just listed) has *not* been accompanied by those anti-terrorist measures desired by a number of politicians, who want states to deal with terorists as they used to deal with *pirates*. Although the international community does consider terrorists heinous and abhorrent and a constant danger to the common good, just as pirates were, it has not gone so far as to allow *any* state to capture and punish them, *wherever* they might be. Should this happen, even if the rule were qualified by numerous exceptions, it could legitimize *violence against anyone* and encourage the spread of armed conflict throughout the world.

THE NECESSARY PREMISES FOR AN ADEQUATE 'RESPONSE' TO TERRORISM

At the present stage, the international community has adopted a primarily 'repressive' attitude to terrorism. Terrorism is seen as an evil that must be suppressed or weeded out, either by forestalling the attacks of terrorist groups, or by capturing and punishing the terrorists through single strikes or the concerted efforts of states. Many states have never seriously considered the historical background and political motives underlying the phenomenon and I shall consider in chapter 8 the consequences of this.

Further, many Western governments make the mistake of considering terrorism as, basically, yet another facet of the struggle between East and West. Whether consciously or unconsciously, explicitly or tacitly, things are still seen as part of the 'enemy brothers' struggle – as Raymond Aron so aptly called it – between two opposing blocs: since neither bloc is homogeneous, each 'brother' tries to instigate disorder and revolution in the other sibling's 'empire'. Within this framework, the United States, especially, has tended to believe (at least until quite recently; an interview given by the late William Casey, then head of the CIA, seems to signal a turning point in this attitude) that the other superpower foments or directs terrorism by remote control, or sends its 'cutthroat retainers' to do so. Hence every terrorist movement is connected to a sovereign state (Libya, Syria, Iran, etc.), which in turn is operating on behalf of a greater power in the opposite camp.

In my opinion, however true this analysis may have been in the past (because the two 'enemy brothers' did behave in the manner described, and the USSR in particular tended to help many a movement that aimed at upsetting the stability of states in the other bloc), today terrorism is resorted to by non-state groups which, although they often receive money and other forms of help from sovereign states, tend to slip from their control. The terrorist phenomenon should be seen within the framework of the progressive *decline* of nation-states and, especially, within that of the slow disintegration of communities into smaller groups, sub-groups and minorities. A solution to the problem could be a *concerted* effort of large, middle-sized and even small powers taking into account the 'ideals' and aspirations of those groups and of the minorities, within the wider context of long-term global solutions.

2

The Exemplary Character of the *Achille Lauro* Incident

THE CASE AS AN ILLUSTRATION OF CURRENT TRENDS IN THE WORLD COMMUNITY

With the world reduced to an ocean of violence and mankind beset by ever increasing perils, the *Achille Lauro* affair is remarkable less for what actually happened than for the new trends in international relations it revealed. This is an exemplary case, in more senses than one. It shows how fragile our lives are: even a pleasure cruise may prove to be fraught with danger, violence spilling over from a world of conflict. Although we try to protect ourselves from the lurking Furies, we still find them lying in wait in the most unforeseen places. Like Prince Prospero, in Poe's story, wishing to flee the 'red death' – the plague that was spreading through the land – we try to barricade ourselves into a fortified abbey to avoid contamination. The prince and his court feel safe until the 'red death' creeps, unnoticed, into a masked ball, dressed as a ghost, and by the end of the feast has overcome all those who thought they had found sanctuary there.

The *Achille Lauro* incident also shows how, when more or less 'private' groups (such as terrorist organizations, unrecognized national liberation movements and the like) carry out violent attacks, it can provoke sovereign states into becoming similarly violent. On both sides there are those who prefer the brusque use of force to the channels of political diplomacy. Some readers may object that violence has existed ever since the world began. That is undeniable. However, it has of late come to be used as an easy way out, preferred by an ever increasing number of domestic and international 'actors'. The impression is that those who have a role to play on the international scene, or who would like to be given a part, are losing their tempers: exasperation and impatience make them opt for the use of force as the most expedient solution. Mediation and negotiation are considered too ponderous and slow. Fortunately there are still some international subjects, as well as private groups, that believe in compromise and conciliation. They do not try to tackle the various causes of violence head on – in itself a difficult feat – but try to examine and discuss them, in the hope that a greater understanding of these causes will help to remove them in the not too distant future. As we shall see, these two very different attitudes to violence are fully revealed in the *Achille Lauro* affair.

The incident also shows how complex and intertwined human relations are today: the ship was Italian with passengers of diverse nationalitites, the terrorists were Palestinians and the affair involved several nations (Egypt, Italy, the United States and, to a lesser extent, the Federal Republic of Germany). Besides, the news of the hijacking was transmitted to the world by a radio station in Göteborg in Sweden.

THE NOVELTY OF THE CASE

The *Achille Lauro* incident also contains a new element that is well worth examining.

Crimes committed within a state, not to mention those that involve various states and concern the whole international community, are extremely hard to reconstruct after the event. This is a point that a distinguished international lawyer, Jean Salmon, made a few years ago, when he underscored how easy it is for states to 'manipulate' the facts in almost all international disputes, simply because there is no international police force to sniff out the evidence, and often there are not even courts to piece together the various bits of the puzzle. In a nutshell, international 'incidents' are like a Pirandello play, with each actor giving his or her version of the facts and the spectator quite powerless to judge which version is closest to the truth. Furthermore, the *dramatis personae* often squabble and disagree over the rules of behaviour that apply, what exactly these rules say, how they should be interpreted, and even whether they apply at all.

By contrast, the *Achille Lauro* case seems an answer to the international lawyer's prayer, since there have been numerous official reconstructions of the facts, made by very influential persons. The Italian Prime Minister, Bettino Craxi, made a detailed report to the Chamber of Deputies on 17 October 1985, after the hijacking had provoked a crisis in the government. About a year later, his diplomatic adviser (who had been directly involved in the affair) published an official account of the more controversial facts (already described, though in more succinct terms, by Craxi). Various other protagonists, American, Egyptian and Italian, have also made long statements to the press, in some cases adding details that help to complete the picture. Recently, the ship's captain, Gerardo De Rosa, published a book of recollections and comments that also contains some new facts. More important still, the voices of politicians have been overtaken by the voice of justice: a long trial was held in Genoa of three of the hijackers and two accomplices. Thus the Court of Assizes was able to question the accused, examine witnesses, collect evidence and then deliver a judgment expressing the judicial version of the hijacking (the rest of the incident did not concern the court). Other judgments were later handed down when the Juvenile Court, followed by the Juvenile Court of Appeal, convicted the youngest hijacker, who was a minor at the time of the incident. A few months later, the Appellate Court of Assizes reviewed the decision of the Court of Assizes.

Hence, the *Achille Lauro* incident is exceptional in that it allows one to make some sense out of the usual tangle of events. This means one can get a rare insight into how states choose between alternatives and the various justifications they advance for their actions, both at the time and after the event.

It would be a pity to waste such a unique occasion to get at the facts and to understand the behaviour, not only of states, but also of non-state bodies, such as the PLO and its various sub-groupings.

THE MAJOR ISSUES RAISED BY THE AFFAIR

Before I summarize the main events of the 'incident', I would like to indicate the principal problems I intend to discuss. Above all, I propose to deal with the way states involved in the 'affair' respected, or failed to respect, the international community's legal standards on terrorism. I shall examine to what extent these states followed the dictates of those standards, and why. Whenever they deviated from them, I shall endeavour to comprehend their reasons and shall consider whether such deviations 'paid off' in psychological, political or diplomatic terms. My reflections on whether or not a state respected those standards are not intended as either an indictment or an exoneration. Rather, my aim is to understand the *various alternatives* from which states can choose during a crisis triggered by terrorist action, and the reasons why they fix upon one choice and not another. From this point of view, I shall try to learn more about how *domestic* factors (political conditions at home, public opinion, national interests, etc.) interact with *international* factors, such as pre-existing links with other states, a desire for hegemony in certain 'areas', the need to take into account the foreign policy of other countries and the strategies they adopt in moments of crisis. It would also be interesting to examine whether the courses of conduct envisaged by international law to deal with terrorism are *practical and realistic*, or whether they are so noble and ambitious as to be beyond the reach of states – at least whenever they are under great pressure, or when innocent lives are at stake.

My ultimate aim is to examine a case *in vitro* (that is, to train my microscope on a specific episode, which offers a whole mass of data that are not normally available) to show to what extent the rules states have created to order, as far as possible, their own future behaviour in cases of terrorism and predict the behaviour of others, do indeed determine they way nations act. Further, when these rules are ignored, I would like to study how the victims of these violations react, and what means they have of mending the torn fabric of international relations.

There is one other aspect of the crisis which is, I feel, significant: as I indicated before, various Italian courts (the Court of Assizes and the Juvenile Court of Genoa, each followed by an Appellate Court) were able to examine at least some aspects of the affair, and gave their verdicts on the actions of the men who had committed the act of terrorism. It would be useful to inquire how the judges faced the issue; above all, to what extent was their *point of view* different from that of the executive, which had to act in the heat of the moment and take decisions on how to deal with the hijacking, as well as on other issues? Did the work of these courts *shed new light* on the dynamics of the events and on their sequence, as well as on the motives underlying the actions of the non-state actors? To what extent were the courts swayed by international legal standards? Was their judgment based exclusively on Italian criminal law, or did they also consider other standards of behaviour? Finally, what was their attitude to terrorism; did they see it as a barbarous phenomenon that must be crushed – by meting out severe punishment to those who conceive terrorist plans – or as a deplorable and very serious problem, no doubt, but one with historical, political and social roots that must not be overlooked before delivering harsh, yet humane, verdicts against the terrorists?

Plainly, by tackling these issues, we are bound to face the vast and delicate question of how *municipal courts* 'interfere' in *international relations* and of whether state judges may, sometimes, play a 'supplementing' or 'surrogating' role for an international legal system that is still so full of loopholes and incomplete. In other words, we will be dealing with relations between the judiciary, the executive and international affairs.

I hope to show that the *Achille Lauro* affair has helped to bring this issue into sharper focus. There is a whole range of 'lessons' to be drawn from the incident, which those who follow the daily events of the world community should not overlook.

3

Facts and Issues

The whole *Achille Lauro* affair, including its immediate sequel on Italian soil, lasted no more than a week: from 7 to 12 October 1985. But during that one week, crammed with unforeseen and dangerous events, both the lives of the hostages and peace itself hung by a thread. Besides, the incidents of that week reverberated through the lives of various states: Egypt hovered on the brink of a political crisis, after having been humiliated on the international scene; in Italy the hijacking created such tensions in the cabinet that the five-party coalition government seemed about to fall apart, though fortunately this danger was averted at the eleventh hour; the United States was first swept by impotent fury at the murder of one of its citizens, then by euphoria that its fighter planes had carried the day – from a military point of view at least the operation had been a success. Not only the public, but Congress as well (which on 19 October 1985 passed a joint resolution), were jubilant that their country had taught a lesson to those fainthearted states that felt reluctant to deal firmly with the affair.

The circumstances of that week form a complex pattern of facts, intertwined with both domestic and international actions, making it difficult to find a thread of logic through the labyrinth. This, of course, is true of all grave international incidents that involve several states. I do, however, feel it is possible to see a pattern in the events of that week and thus divide the whole affair into various episodes.

THE HIJACKING

On 7 October 1985, at 1.15 p.m., four members of a faction of
the PLO, the Palestine Liberation Front (PLF) – itself
divided into three sub-groups – took command of the *Achille
Lauro*, an Italian transatlantic liner, at about ten nautical miles
from the coast of Egypt, while it was sailing from Alexandria
to Port Said.

The ship was fairly full: there were about 201 passengers on
board, including 52 Swiss, 29 Austrians, 28 Italians, 5 British,
12 Americans and 11 citizens of the Federal Republic of
Germany. About 600 passengers had (fortunately for them) left
the ship at Alexandria for a trip to the pyramids, expecting to
rejoin her in Port Said – these, I imagine, included the only
two Israelis on the cruise. Also on board were 344 members of
the crew, many of these being so-called 'transit passengers':
staff who are not part of the crew in a strict sense, such as
waiters, members of the band, dancers and other performers.
Their presence is hardly surprising since the *Achille Lauro* was
on a pleasure cruise.

News of the hijacking was transmitted by the ship's radio at
2 p.m. and picked up by the coastal station in Göteborg, in
Sweden; however the name of the ship was not given, it was
merely announced that an Italian vessel had been captured by
armed Palestinians.

Only after it was all over, on the afternoon of Wednesday 9
October, did it become known that there were only four
hijackers, though they were extremely aggressive and very
heavily armed. Another point that was not clear at the
beginning was the 'political area' to which the terrorists
belonged. A few hours after the hijacking, they threatened to
kill the passengers, starting with the Americans, unless the
Israeli government released 50 Palestinians from prison,
among these Sami Al Quantari, whom they referred to as 'the
great man from Naharia' (because he had carried out an act of
terrorism in Naharia in Israel and had then been taken

prisoner by the Israeli armed forces). This specific request was the only clue to the fact that the hijackers were Palestinians. But to which faction of the PLO did they belong?

What actually happened was that the passengers and crew were forced at gunpoint to descend in single file from the restaurant (where most of them were when the hijacking began) into the main saloon, known as the 'tapestry saloon'. The hijackers then brought in several jerry cans of kerosene and said they would set them alight at the first sign of insubordination among the hostages.

All this took some time: roughly three hours. The hijackers then told the captain, De Rosa, to sail for the Syrian port of Tartus and then – as I have already said –. to transmit a message over the ship's radio containing their requests.

After setting sail for Tartus, they asked the captain to point out the Israeli, American and British passengers, and to separate them from the others. After checking through the passenger list and muster roll, twenty American and British nationals were picked out (according to the captain 'four or five others managed to escape recognition, claiming to be Austrians or Australians and that they did not have their passports with them'). However, the hijackers insisted on singling out the Jews; again according to the captain's report 'they [the Palestinians] did not care whether the Jews were Israeli. They intended to single them out even if they were the nationals of other countries. Italians, for example.' Fortunately 'there were only a couple left on board', and one of them carried an American diplomatic passport. De Rosa managed to keep this from the terrorists, just as he managed to persuade them that the Portuguese singer who, the previous evening, had sung an Israeli song, was not Jewish. It would appear that, thanks to the efforts of the captain, the 'Jew hunt' produced no victims. The hijackers had to rest content with their hand-picked band of American and British passengers.

Meanwhile, in the outside world – in Italy, in the United States, in Egypt and in the other states concerned – governments, or their 'crisis committees', were convening. They were faced with a difficult task, because as I have already said it was not yet known who the terrorists were, nor to which political group they belonged. All they knew was that the terrorists' requests had been addressed to Israel, and that the lives of all the passengers were in very great danger.

Naturally, one of the most active was the Italian government. It decided at once to follow two simultaneous courses of action: to be in *contact* with all the interested states and with the PLO, to try to achieve a solution to the crisis that would save hundreds of innocent lives on board the *Achille Lauro*; and at the same time to make plans for *military action* as a last resort. Thus the Italian government not only got in touch with the United States and the Federal Republic of Germany, but also with various Arab countries with which it had friendly relations (Egypt, Jordan, Syria and Tunisia), and Israel. It also sent urgent messages to Yasser Arafat, requesting him to clarify his own position. On that very Monday, the PLO issued a statement from Tunis asserting that 'it had no part in, and dissociated itself from, the hijacking, condemning it as an act of sabotage against its own peace efforts.' As Craxi announced in the Chamber of Deputies on 17 October, 'the American authorities themselves, on the night of October 7, expressly requested the Italian government to ask Arafat to announce publicly he had no part in the act of terrorism.' This the PLO leader did in the early hours of Tuesday 8 October when he reiterated his denunciation of the hijacking of the Italian liner, 'offering his services to work for a peaceful solution, that is, one that would leave all the passengers unharmed' (as Craxi put it in his speech).

At the same time the Italians took care to inform the appropriate *international forums*. On 8 October, the Italian representative to the United Nations, Maurizio Bucci, officially requested the President of the UN Security Council to bring the hijacking to the Council's attention, 'with a view to firmly condemning such an act and to appealing for the prompt liberation of the hostages.' A similar request was made by the Austrian Foreign Minister and then, on the following day, also by the permanent representative for Greece. By 8 October the UN Secretary General, Xavier Pérez de Cuéllar, had made a public declaration condemning the act of terrorism. The Security Council itself – which was then examining the difficult Middle Eastern question – did not have to make any declaration because, on 9 October, Mr Bucci informed the President that the hostages had been freed. None the less, the Council did issue a condemnation of the act of terrorism (a declaration that was read out by the President in the name of all fifteen members).

Let us now turn to the *plans for military action*. These were set in motion at once. On Monday night and on Tuesday, Italian military units left for Akrotiri, a British military base on Cyprus which the United Kingdom had put at their disposal. The Italian task force was made up of sixty paratroopers from the 'Col Moschin' battalion, later joined by a naval 'raiding party' (from the 'Teseo Tesei' group), by four HH–3F helicopters and by various military experts, who had studied the *Achille Lauro's* design to prepare plans for a surprise attack on the ship. Fortunately, the task force did not intervene: in their forecast of casualties during an eventual attack, on the presumption that there were at least a dozen terrorists aboard, the experts had anticipated at least twenty deaths among the assailants and the hostages.

SYRIA IS ASKED TO MEDIATE AND KLINGHOFFER IS MURDERED

The *Achille Lauro* reached Tartus at 11 a.m. on Tuesday 8 October. At first the hijackers wanted the ship to sail to within a mile and a half of the coast, but changed their minds when the captain explained that the ship could run aground there. The ship hove to at about seven miles from the shore.

No sooner had they arrived than it became obvious that the Syrians were not prepared to negotiate, or, at least, that they were not favourably disposed *a priori* towards the hijackers. As De Rosa said in his report '... something unexpected and sinister happened. The ships that lay at anchor suddenly sailed away, obviously after receiving an order to that effect from land. In no time at all we were alone: the sea around us was completely empty.'

After a while there was an exchange of messages, via radio, between the hijackers and the Syrian authorities. Since it was all in Arabic, no one on board could understand a word. All Captain De Rosa could make out was that, as time went by and the discussions over the air went on, the tone of the hijackers changed from euphoric, to irritated, to angry and then even to 'furious'. Later the Court of Assizes in Genoa made a partial reconstruction of these exchanges, based partly on fragmentary recordings and partly on the evidence given by some of the hijackers: the latter wanted the Syrians to mediate between them and the British and American consuls, as well as the International Committee of the Red Cross. Apparently, the hijackers wanted the two consuls to come on board for talks; if these talks led nowhere – because the two respective governments refused to ask Israel to free the 50 Palestinians – all the hostages would be killed. As so often happens in these cases, the hijackers gave differing accounts of the facts. According to what Al Asker Bassam, one of the terrorists, told De Rosa on reaching Tartus, they had originally intended to land with only the American and British hostages, leaving the ship and the other passengers free.

At one stage the Palestinians ordered the American and British passengers and members of the crew to mount the round plaform that served as a roof for the tapestry saloon. Nineteen people (excluding Leon Klinghoffer, who stayed below because he was confined to a wheel-chair and could not be hauled on to the platform) were forced to stand for many hours, out in the open, on a space ten metres in diameter. According to De Rosa, their purpose was twofold: they wanted their likely victims to be within full view, having already told the Syrians they were all British and Americans; they also wanted to prevent any attack from the air (the platform was the only area on which a helicopter could have landed).

After a few hours, it became absolutely clear that the Syrians refused to cooperate in any way. In reality, the Syrians had immediately contacted the governments of Italy and the United States to ask if they were prepared to negotiate. On receiving negative replies from both Rome and Washington, Damascus refused the liner permission to berth in the port of Tartus and, at the same time, publicly condemned the hijacking. This was something the terrorists had not foreseen.

The terrorists were so incensed by the Syrians' refusal to cooperate that tension in the group reached a high pitch. It was then (at 3 p.m. on 8 October) that the leader, Al Molqi, disappeared for about a quarter of an hour, returning to De Rosa carrying two American passports (one of which belonged to Leon Klinghoffer) and 'indicated the figure one by holding up a finger'. At that moment – according to the judges in Genoa – Captain De Rosa noticed bloodstains on Al Molqi's left shoe and trouser leg and 'from that moment and in that precise context, he [De Rosa] became aware of the murder' of Klinghoffer. This is borne out by what De Rosa himself wrote in his 'personal account'.

Why did the hijackers kill Klinghoffer, an old man in a wheel-chair, who should have aroused their pity (if they had been less fanatical)? Later, De Rosa did advance some conjectures that seem fairly plausible; all the more so since he was in direct contact with the terrorists for so many hours and spoke several times to the youngest of the group. The captain believes that a determining factor was that '[Klinghoffer] embodied two of the most execrable faults in the eyes of the terrorists for he was both Jewish and American.' But he felt that there were other contributing factors. First, the fact that Klinghoffer was confined to his wheel-chair and could not be moved about easily had incensed and envenomed the terrorists. Second, the fact that he had been parted from the other British and American passengers allowed the Palestinians to kill him unbeknown to the rest: the terrorists wanted to carry out their plan of killing some hostages to force the various states involved to give in to their blackmail; at the same time they

were afraid they might set off an uncontrollable chain reaction
in the crew and passengers (reasonable fears given the dis-
proportion in number: 545 against 4). This may explain the
'stealthy' killing of Klinghoffer, running counter to the logic
of terrorism, which usually gives the murder of hostages as
much publicity as possible.

Having killed one American passenger, the hijackers
hesitated for some time before they ordered De Rosa to
transmit a message over the air announcing that two hostages
had already been killed: the interested states must make haste
if they did not want the number of victims to increase as time
ticked away. They then made the British and American
passengers come down from the platform and at, 4.40 p.m.,
they ordered the crew to up anchor and sail for Libya.

Naturally, the 'crisis committees' in the various capitals
were thrown off balance by the news: several countries
(including Italy and the United States) began to make new
plans for an armed attack on the hijackers.

At this point the strategies adopted by the governments of
Italy and the United States diverged. Without abandoning its
'military option', Italy threw all its energies into an attempt to
find a peaceful solution. Italy's hand had been strengthened by
the political isolation of the hijackers (both Syria and Libya
had condemned the hijacking of the *Achille Lauro*) and by
Arafat's willingness to cooperate in apprehending the hijackers; it therefore decided to try for a 'political' solution to
the crisis. On the other hand, Maxwell Rabb, the US
ambassador in Rome, had been instructed by Ronald Reagan
to inform Craxi that 'his Government felt the situation was
intolerable; he confirmed the Administration in Washington
was completely averse to taking part in any form of negotiation';
he also informed Craxi 'of the [United States'] decision to
initiate military action, which the Americans had decided
should start no later than Wednesday night [8–9 October]'.
Finally, the ambassador told Craxi his government wished to
carry out its military operation 'alone, should any divergence
emerge as to the necessity for it'. Craxi disagreed, politely but

firmly; he stressed the fact that the ship was Italian (thereby indicating that he felt that only his own government could act militarily, should the need arise); he then pointed out that news of the killing of two hostages and the threat to murder others had never been confirmed; lastly, he stressed that the time was ripe for negotiation.

The United States government then felt obliged to hold back. Meanwhile, the lines of communication between the Italian Prime Minister, the Italian Foreign Office, Egypt and the PLO ran hot. A turning point was reached on Tuesday 8 October in the late evening.

THE NEGOTIATIONS IN CAIRO

While the *Achille Lauro* was sailing full steam towards Libya, the hijackers, who were listening to the news on the radio, suddenly became 'euphoric'. At 7.20 on Tuesday evening they ordered De Rosa to change course and head for Port Said. Explaining that a man called Abu Khaled (in fact it was Abul Abbas) was taking part in the negotiations, they also asserted he was Arafat's emissary.

As the liner was sailing towards Port Said, Arafat's 'emissary' had indeed arrived in Cairo. With the representative of the PLO in the Egyptian capital seated beside him, he spoke over the air to the hijackers.

The *Achille Lauro* arrived at Port Said at dawn on 9 October and cast anchor at 7.30 a.m., 15 miles from the coast. At this point the radio messages between the terrorists and Abul Abbas came thick and fast.

This was also perhaps the moment when – according to the facts ascertained by the judges in Genoa, and to De Rosa's account – the hijackers stated that their original intention had been to take advantage of the liner's arrival in the Israeli port of Ashdod, to land and carry out a massacre, and 'then return on board'. They had to abandon this plan because some passengers, or a member of the crew, had noticed that they had arms in their cabin. To avoid arrest, the Palestinians had taken over the whole ship, although the hijacking had not been foreseen in the original plan.

Let us now go back to the previous night, when an attempt was being made, via international negotiation, to persuade the hijackers to sail for Port Said. By Wednesday morning, Arafat had sent Craxi a message to the effect that 'after all our efforts throughout the night we have managed to bring the ship back into Egyptian waters; we would like to say that we have great confidence that the whole affair will come to a propitious end within the current day.' It is now possible to say – with hindsight – that the tug-of-war between Abul Abbas and Arafat had ended overnight in a victory for the latter.

However, in his message, Arafat requested Italy to 'try to persuade Israel to make at least some form of symbolic gesture': in other words, to comply with the hijackers' demands and release at least a few of the 50 prisoners. But Craxi was unable to do anything about this request; as he told the Chamber on 17 October: 'I felt that we could not comply with this part of the message, since the necessary conditions for making tentative enquiries in this sense did not exist.' At the same time the Italian Government contacted Hans Dietrich Genscher, the German Foreign Minister (who was visiting Jerusalem at the time), and asked him to tell the Israeli Government that it did not intend to comply with Arafat's request.

Later, Arafat sent Craxi another message: the *Achille Lauro* would be released 'with all the passengers safe and well' and with no demands for the release of Palestinians. At the same time, however, Arafat asked Mubarak to guarantee that after the hijackers had been taken prisoner they would be transferred to Tunis, the PLO headquarters, for questioning and for eventual trial. While Abul Abbas was telling the hijackers what to do and, probably, agreeing on a version of what happened on board, to be given to the Egyptian authorities and to the whole world, the Egyptian Foreign Minister was trying to get the other countries involved to concur with the

Mubarak–Arafat agreement. He thus hoped to prevent those nations from any last-minute use of force against the hijackers and, also, to involve them in the agreement, so that they would not try to embarass Egypt with requests for the hijackers' extradition at a later date.

It was, therefore, the Egyptians who initiated the idea of a 'safe-conduct' for the terrorists; an agreement for which they drafted the text, which was then presented for approval to the ambassadors of the United States, the United Kingdom, the Federal Republic of Germany and Italy. The agreement was to the effect that all signatory states promised not to initiate criminal proceedings and not to request the extradition of the hijackers, if the latter freed all the hostages, and to allow the hijackers to be handed over to the PLO. It did not expressly include the proviso that the hijackers had killed no one on board the *Achille Lauro* but, as Mubarak, Craxi and Andreotti were to declare later, all the contracting parties took this point for granted, because they could never have condoned murder on board the liner. In fact at that stage it was not at all apparent, either to public opinion or to the governments anxiously watching from their capitals, whether one, or more, of the hostages had been murdered. Although the leader of the terrorists had announced the murder of two hostages, there were indications that his words were merely a threat, which had never been carried out. When, under pressure from Ambassador Rabb (who was worried about the safety of the US citizens aboard the ship), on the evening of 8 October, Craxi again asked the Egyptians to send him all the details of any possible killings aboard the *Achille Lauro* that their radio stations and secret services had been able to pick up, the reply was a definite statement that no one had been killed. Even at 12.35 on Wednesday 9 October, according to a note from Palazzo Chigi (the seat of the Prime Minister's office), 'we were able to intercept a radio transmission from the *Achille Lauro* on which the hijackers themselves stated that all the passengers were in good health.' Therefore, when the Egyptians, Italians and Germans initialled the agreement to give the hijackers a safe-conduct – at about 3 p.m. on 9 October – they did so in good faith. The American and British ambassadors to Cairo had refused to initial, let alone sign, the agreement, for reasons they were not prepared to disclose.

By 3.30 p.m. that day, the hijacking was all over and an Egyptian tug moved alongside the liner to take off the four hijackers. The nightmare seemed to be over. From on board the tug, an Arab (in fact Abul Abbas) waved to the passengers and said how sorry he was that for the last three days they had been put to such inconvenience.

The anguish suffered by the other passengers had just come to an end, while the mystery of Klinghoffer's murder was just beginning.

NEWS OF KLINGHOFFER'S MURDER IS RELEASED AND THE EGYPTIANS 'TAKE CHARGE' OF THE HIJACKERS

Less than an hour after the Egyptian tug had taken the four Palestinians off the liner, the Italian Foreign Minister rang through to Capitain De Rosa. The latter, 'in a telephone conversation to which the diplomats on the "crisis committee" listened through an amplifier, stated that: (a) he had regained complete control of his ship [which still lay at anchor 15 miles from Port Said]; (b) the hijackers had abandoned the ship; (c) the passengers were all well' (according to the note from Palazzo Chigi, quoted earlier). Everywhere there was jubilation that the whole affair had ended and, at the time, it seemed justified. As Craxi prepared to receive journalists for a news conference on the latest developments, he felt understandably gratified. No doubts lingered in his mind that any passengers might have been killed; earlier reports had also come from Egypt saying that all the passengers were alive and well. Was it then a vague fear, a premonition, or the scrupulousness of a man who will leave no stone unturned, that made him make one last check? At 6.10 p.m. he telephoned De Rosa, a few minutes before the news conference.

On that occasion, though not in very clear terms, the captain gave the Prime Minister the sad news of Klinghoffer's murder, which Craxi immediately conveyed to the press.

One wonders why De Rosa, who – according to what emerged in the Genoa trial and to what he himself has written – had realized as early as Tuesday afternoon that Klinghoffer had been killed, lied to Andreotti in his telephone conversation on Wednesday at 4.20 p.m., only to admit the truth to Craxi a few hours later. The puzzle remains unresolved, since the Genoa court did not explain the reasons for De Rosa's behaviour; nor should it have done so, since the point was hardly relevant to its decision on the hijacking and the murder of Klinghoffer. It appears that De Rosa was afraid of possible 'reprisals', or other acts, by the hijackers, so long as they were aboard or close to the ship. Once he was absolutely certain they had disembarked, he made a statement about what had really happened, at least to Craxi. Why then, at 6 p.m. on Thursday (a day after the hijackers had left the ship), did he make an official statement to the Italian consul in Port Said in which, as he told the court in Genoa, he omitted to mention all the facts about the murder known to him, which he was later to describe at the preliminary inquiry [in Genoa], merely declaring 'that the American passenger had died'? Clearly, he either did not wish to cause the Egyptian authorities any further embarrassment, or was being excessively prudent, or he wanted to avoid any further complications for his passengers on the liner – which now lay at anchor in Port Said, and was therefore under the direct control of the Egyptians; once again the Italian captain chose to be cautious and reticent, deciding perhaps that half-truths were better in the circumstances than the whole truth.

Equally strange was the behaviour of the Egyptian authorities. Despite Craxi's announcement of 6.30 p.m. on Wednesday the Egyptian Government replied at 8.55 p.m. to an enquiry by the Italian Ministry of Defence, stating that 'there had been no killings on board the *Achille Lauro*' (from the note from Palazzo Chigi). According to a note of 14 October 1985 from the Italian embassy in Cairo, quoted during the trial in Genoa, 'the public prosecutor in Port Said – for reasons of a political, domestic and international nature – had directed the inquiries so as to show that the criminal acts had taken place neither in Egyptian, nor in Italian territorial waters, but in Syrian territorial waters.' For the same reasons, in the earliest phase of his inquiry, he took care to hush up the murder, investigating the disappearance of a man, rather than looking for his body. (The embassy note goes on to remark that the public prosecutor had justified his behaviour with the words: 'One man's death is a terrible thing, but it is nothing compared to the safety of 400 human beings . . .')

The behaviour of the Egyptians (which I shall examine in greater detail later on, in my analysis of Egypt's attitude to the whole affair) seems to have been inspired by a single-minded desire to deny, suppress or play down Klinghoffer's murder, so as to respect the 'safe-conduct agreement' and get the four hijackers off their hands as soon as possible. Later, I will show that there were legal and political reasons for the Egyptian authorities' 'ostrich-like tactics'.

Once the four hijackers had landed, the two PLO representatives 'took them in charge'. Instead of leaving instantly for Tunis, they stayed on in Cairo, in an unknown hideout, from Wednesday afternoon until they finally departed in the late evening on Thursday. During the news blackout on the hijackers' whereabouts, Craxi had announced 'Italy's intention to ask Egypt to extradite the four hijackers so that they might be subjected to a fair trial in Italy. In case the hijackers had already been transferred into PLO custody' Craxi 'sent Yasser Arafat a request to hand them over to Italy' (from Craxi's speech of 17 October 1985). President Reagan was promptly informed of 'Italy's intentions', with the assurance 'that everything would be attempted, within the scope of Italy's concrete options, to discover and punish the guilty parties' (from the same speech).

Nevertheless, Egypt continued to sit on the fence, and surreptitiously transferred the four hijackers, together with the two PLO representatives (one of them being Abul Abbas), some Egyptian civil servants and ten armed guards, on to an Egyptian Boeing 737 bound for Tunis.

THE INTERMINABLE NIGHT AT SIGONELLA

The Egyptian aircraft never reached Tunis. The authorities there had, at first, given their consent; they then changed their minds and refused the plane permission to enter Tunisian airspace. There may have been several reasons for this: Tunisia wished to avoid giving the PLO factions a chance to 'settle their accounts'; perhaps, too, remembering the Israeli attack on 1 October 1985, they did not want the hijackers' presence on Tunisian soil to provoke another air-raid; above all, American pressure was a decisive factor, as both sides were to admit later. (The Americans declared that their main aim was to prevent the terrorists from finding a safe refuge anywhere.)

The aircraft changed course and headed for Greece, but Athens also refused to allow it to land. The plane was flying back towards Cairo (a formal statement to this effect was made by the Egyptian Foreign Minister on 11 October) when, under specific orders from President Reagan, four fighter planes left the US aircraft-carrier *Saratoga*, intercepted the Egyptian Boeing 737 and forced it to make for the NATO base of Sigonella, in Sicily (a few kilometres from Catania). Before they could all land they needed Italian consent; thus Reagan rang Craxi to make this request at midnight. The permission was granted, as the Prime Minister later explained to the Chamber of Deputies, 'because the circumstances were exceptional, and also in order to pursue our principal aim of capturing, if possible, the authors of the very serious incidents of the preceding days [the hijacking] and of grave misdeeds, including the almost certain perpetration of a murder on board the *Achille Lauro*'. However, although the Egyptian plane landed at Sigonella, the four fighter planes from the *Saratoga* did not. Instead, two US military transport C141 planes carrying troops arrived to meet the Egyptian plane. As soon as the Boeing landed, it was surrounded by 50 Italian soldiers serving at the base; these, in turn, were surrounded by 50 American soldiers 'armed and ready' – members of the so-called Delta Force – that had just landed with the two C141s under the command of General Carl W. Stiner, who was receiving his orders direct from Washington over the radio. His instructions from the White House were to 'arrest the terrorists' and take them to the United States. What followed was a tug-of-war between the Italians and the Americans. Craxi explained to Reagan, who was insisting that the Delta Force should complete its mission, that this was out of the question. On 17 October, Craxi told the Chamber that Italy's 'legal stance' was that 'the crimes had been committed in international waters, on board an Italian vessel, and should therefore be considered criminal acts perpetrated on Italian territory', adding that 'the Italian Government could not, by its own decision, remove those responsible for the hijacking of the *Achille Lauro* from the jurisdiction of the Italian court'. (One cannot help remarking that this statement was somewhat at variance with the government's attitude when it concluded the safe-conduct agreement.) Behind this barrage of legal arguments, there was of course Italy's resentment at its 'Big Brother's' show of arrogance. Reagan was forced to give in. To sugar the pill he had to swallow, he announced there and then that he would request the terrorists' extradition later on, adding that, in his opinion, the Italians ought to arrest not only the four hijackers, but also the two PLO representatives travelling with them. Craxi disagreed, though his refusal, this time, was less categorical: the Italians would make 'inquiries' about the two Palestinians.

It is worth noting here that the legal arguments that served formally to justify Craxi's political decision not to give in to the Americans' insistence also helped Reagan to explain his 'retreat' to the US public. Indeed, during his press conference on 11 October at the White House, when asked about his 'alleged disagreement' with Craxi, Reagan replied:

[during my telephone conversation with Craxi] he told me what his situation was with regard to them, and I told him what ours was. And I told him that we would introduce an extradition request. He told me what their legal process was with regard to that, that it wasn't something that he could just give me an opinion on himself, any more than I could if the situation was reversed.

Having dampened, for the time being, the Americans' eagerness to take justice into their own hands, the Italian government still had to deal with the Egyptians and the Palestinians. The former agreed to hand over the four hijackers (who were escorted off the plane and arrested by the Italian police at 5 a.m. on Friday 11 October). However, when the Italian judicial officials requested that the two PLO representatives also be handed over for questioning, they were informed by the Egyptians that the PLO representatives refused to leave the aircraft. The Italian judge and police could not themselves board the Boeing 737 without being authorized to do so by the Egyptians, because – as the latter explained and as Craxi himself emphasized during his speech to the Chamber – the aircraft was 'on a special mission for the Egyptian government' and enjoyed 'extraterritorial rights'. Negotiations dragged on through the whole of that Friday. Meanwhile, between 5 a.m. and late that same evening, the Italian judicial officials had identified the four hijackers and Craxi had sent a diplomatic envoy (his personal adviser, Antonio Badini) to Sigonella. The envoy was allowed to board the aircraft and talk to Abul Abbas. (An account of this conversation was published later on and shows how the Palestinian leader systematically lied in reply to all Badini's questions.)

At 8.15 p.m. on Friday 11 October, the public prosecutor from Syracuse 'felt the magistrates were satisfied with their inquiries and declared that the aircraft had permission to leave

Sigonella'. The plane took off for Rome, with the two
Palestinians and the Egyptians still on board. Even though, as
Craxi said later to the Chamber, 'as from that moment the
legal grounds for detaining the Egypt-Air plane and its
passengers no longer existed', the Italian Government agreed
with its counterpart in Egypt that the aircraft should fly from
Sigonella to Ciampino airport, Rome; this was to allow the
Italians 'to explore the possibility of making further inquiries',
in line with what Craxi had promised Reagan. Thus, at 10.01
p.m., the plane took off for Ciampino.

There is one important point, to which I should now like to
draw attention, which helps to explain in part the reasons that
lay behind the Italians' behaviour. While the Boeing was at
Sigonella and the Italians and Americans were having their
tug-of-war, the *Achille Lauro* still lay at anchor in Port Said, in
Egyptian territorial waters. True, many passengers had been
allowed to disembark, many of them Americans who had
immediately appealed to their embassy in Cairo for protection.
Nevertheless, in fact the liner was, more or less, a prisoner of
the Egyptians. The latter were merely applying the international rules on foreign ships in a state's territorial waters and
refusing to allow the *Achille Lauro* to leave for Italy.

THE AMERICANS TRY TO FORCE THE ITALIANS' HAND

The Americans must have been concerned and upset by the
plane's departure: three minutes later a US military aircraft
took off from the NATO base, without authorization, and
followed the Egyptian Boeing. (According to *Time*'s careful
reconstruction of the facts, *another* American aircraft also took
off to 'tail' the Egyptian plane: this was a T39, carrying
General Stiner who had boarded the plane in great haste.) The
Italians seemed to have been expecting this move, since the
moment the Egyptian Boeing departed, four Italian fighter
planes also took off from the military base in Giolia del Colle
(near Bari) 'to protect it during flight' (as Craxi put it in his

speech to the Chamber); but protect it from whom, if not from the only foreign state which had aircraft in Italy and which could have been interested in diverting the Egyptian plane elsewhere? It appears that the government intended this 'escort' to play a dual role: to reassure the *Americans* that the Egyptian plane would not be allowed to return to Egypt; and to reassure the *Egyptians* that the Americans would not intercept the plane again.

Let us return to the planes in flight for Rome. According to Craxi's account of the episode 'the [American] pilot did not answer our fighters' requests for identification; indeed, he asked them to move off.' At 40 km from Ciampino, the American plane (an F14, according to the Italian pilots) disappeared from the radar screens. The Egyptian Boeing landed at Ciampino at about 11 p.m. and, in Craxi's words, 'a few seconds later, a US military T39 plane landed a dozen or so metres away and declared an emergency.' (This was the plane on which the furious General Stiner was travelling.) Italy immediately sent a note of protest to Washington. It is not known exactly when the American aircraft took off again.

The next day the Americans tried another approach, a little less bumptious and futile. At dawn on 12 October (at 5.30 a.m. to be exact) Ambassador Rabb rang the doorbell of Mr Salvatore Zhara Buda, the *chef de cabinet* to the Italian Minister of Justice, to hand him a request for the 'provisional arrest' of Abul Abbas, having received a warrant for his arrest signed by a Judge of the Court of the District of Columbia; it was asserted in the request that the Palestinian was seriously implicated in the hijacking. In particular, Rabb wanted Abul Abbas to be kept 'in custody', in accordance with the 1983 bilateral treaty on extradition, since a 'formal request for extradition' was being sent from the United States. The American note was at once transmitted by the Italian authorities to the public prosecutor's offices in Genoa and Syracuse (those that had claimed jurisdiction in the matter).

On the same Saturday, a few hours after Rabb's unexpected visit to Mr Zhara Buda, the latter was summoned to Palazzo

Chigi, together with three judges from the Ministry of Justice. They were required to read carefully through the documents provided by the Americans and to give their *fully independent* opinions thereon. The three judges withdrew and later handed their conclusions to the Prime Minister and to the Minister of Justice: in their opinion the documents furnished by the Americans were entirely insufficient to justify a 'provisional arrest' of Abul Abbas under the terms of the 1983 treaty.

Still on Saturday 12 October, at midday, the public prosecutor's office of the Rome Court of Appeal received a telegram from the public prosecutor in Syracuse 'in which it was asserted that no further measures need to be adopted with regard to the *Achille Lauro* hijacking episode'. According to one of the government officials involved in the affair, this clearly meant that there were no grounds for questioning and therefore for keeping Abbas any longer. The public prosecutor in Genoa also sent to the Italian Ministry of the Interior, at 1.30 p.m. that same Saturday, a telex announcing that 'at this stage there are no sufficient grounds to allow this office to take interim measures against Abul Abbas, for allegedly participating in the hijacking of the ship *Achille Lauro* and in the hostage taking.' The Minister of Justice 'confirmed the unacceptable nature . . . of the US request for a provisional arrest' (from Craxi's speech). At this point, the Italian government allowed the Egyptian aircraft to take off from Fiumicino airport in Rome (to which it had flown from Ciampino). The Egyptian ambassador informed the Italian government that 'for security reasons' (probably to avoid any further interceptions by the US Air Force or to eschew any surprise attacks from the Israeli secret services) the two PLO leaders 'would be leaving Italian territory on board a plane belonging to a Yugoslav airline'. And so they did, at 7.02 p.m. on Saturday 12 October. Once the Egyptian aircraft had left Fiumicino, the authorities in Cairo allowed the *Achille Lauro* to set sail from Port Said.

It is worth noting here that the famous 'information' promised by the Americans did not reach Italy until the *day after* the Palestinians and the Egyptian aircraft had left. In the view of the Genoa Court of Assizes, that information 'seemed then – and, indeed, seems today – very general and totally irrelevant to the trial, as the judge at first instance himself said in his remittal of the case'. Indeed, neither the public prosecutor in Genoa, nor his counterpart in Syracuse, felt that the 'information' was sufficient to issue a warrant for the arrest of Abul Abbas. Such a warrant was issued by the public prosecutor in Syracuse only on 25 October, after the judge at first instance in that town had questioned the four hijackers and made his report.

THE TRIAL IN ITALY

The last phase of the incident was a trial before the Genoa Court of Assizes. Only five (three hijackers and two of their accomplices in Italy) out of the fifteen men accused appeared before the court. The fourth terrorist was only seventeen at the time of the hijacking and had to appear before the Juvenile Court in Genoa. As we shall see in a later chapter, the trial ended with three life sentences in absentia for the terrorists (including Abul Abbas) who were still at large; the others received sentences of varying lengths. A little later, the youngest hijacker was given sixteen years and three months. All these verdicts were confirmed and the sentences slightly increased, in 1987, by the Court of Appeal for Juveniles and the Appellate Court of Assizes. On 10 May 1988 the Court of Cassation reconfirmed all the sentences.

4

The International Agreement to Give the Hijackers a Safe Conduct

AN AGREEMENT IS REACHED

The facts, which I have tried to reconstruct on the basis of reliable eye-witness accounts and statements, seem to indicate that the hijackers were not acting for a state nor for the PLO, but that their orders came from one of the factions of a group within the PLO, called the PLF. These facts, therefore, show that the hijacking – at first glance at least – cannot be attributed directly to a subject of international law. At an international level, this made the negotiations all the more difficult. Sovereign states, or national liberation movements possessing a modicum of international personality, are more appropriate counterparts than tiny, fairly isolated groups. Talks, and certainly negotiations, are far more difficult with these groups. This explains why both Italy and Egypt were in favour of bringing Arafat into the talks, and why Egypt allowed Abul Abbas (who, at this point in the affair, seemed to be acting for and with the approval of the leader of the PLO) to come to Cairo to persuade the hijackers to surrender.

The deal for the 'liberation' of the terrorists was agreed on by the Egyptian Government and Abul Abbas and taken down in writing on 8 October 1985, some time between 1 and 3 p.m. As noted in the previous chapter, it merely stated that the 'group responsible for the action against the Italian ship *Achille Lauro* was to surrender immediately' on two conditions: (a) no request would be advanced for their extradition or punishment, and (b) the PLO would 'take them in charge'. Only the German and Italian Ambassadors, after receiving the approval of their respective ministers, initialled the document drafted by Egypt. Hence, all three signatory states were bound *amongst themselves* not to initiate criminal proceedings against the hijackers; Egypt also committed itself to allowing the hijackers to leave the country for Tunisia (where the PLO had its headquarters).

At this stage I should like to open a long parenthesis, to describe both the singular attitude taken by the Italian Foreign Minister, Mr Giulio Andreotti, and the numerous waverings and contradictions contained in the Egyptian 'version' of the facts. Let us begin by taking a look at Andreotti's statements.

In an interview he gave on 10 October – the day after the agreement had been concluded – on being asked whether it was a written agreement, the minister replied: 'No, not written. It was an agreement put before us by the Egyptian Foreign Minister and, I believe, before other governments.' An amazing statement, since there is proof – quite irrefutable proof, now that the text of the agreement is available – that the agreement was a written one, and internationally binding (even though it was concluded in a 'simplified' form, that is, by being merely initialled or signed).

The statement will puzzle all those who are not familiar with the 'Byzantine' mentality of our elder statesmen. The Italian Foreign Minister's amazing statement should be interpreted as being exclusively political. It was a tactical move, with a twofold objective: first, by saying that the agreement was merely *oral* and *general*, he wished to belittle its significance, so that it would not seem even to require a specific and explicit *ad hoc* authorization; second, he wanted to emphasize that, in any case, it was based on the implicit condition that the hijackers had not murdered or wounded anyone. Since, as shall see, this condition had not been explicitly mentioned in the written text, Andreotti took the opportunity to insist that it had been the basic precondition of that agreement; his statement was intended to justify the Italian actions, to eliminate lingering doubts that the Italian Government had been double-dealing or had naively accepted the conditions of the hijackers. Andreotti's statement allowed Italy to act freely, once it discovered that the famous 'condition' had not been respected by the hijackers.

Equally strange, or rather, equally confused and ambiguous, was the attitude of the Egyptians in 'construing' the facts leading up to this agreement. I shall mention just a few of their fluctuating and contradictory statements. In an interview given on 9 October on American television (reproduced verbatim the next day in the *New York Times*), the Egyptian Ambassador to Washington asserted repeatedly that Egypt had had no part in the safe-conduct agreement, having acted merely as a 'go-between' for the two sides that had entered into it, Italy and the PLO (which was acting for the hijackers). The next day, President Hosni Mubarak presented the facts in similar, though much vaguer, terms: he said that Egypt had indeed helped to draw up the terms of the agreement and had later received the consent of Italy and the PLO thereto. However, the very same day, the Egyptian Foreign Minister, Esmat Abdel Meguid, gave a different version: he insisted that Egypt had cooperated in the drafting of the agreement, but only at the express request of the ambassadors of various nations (United States, Italy, Federal Republic of Germany, France and Great Britain), adding that the agreement was then signed only by the ambassadors of Italy and Germany. Finally, on 11 October, the Egyptian Ministry of Foreign Affairs issued an official note saying that Egypt 'negotiated with the hijackers of the ship on humanitarian grounds. . . .It did so at the insistence of some countries that had nationals on board the ship. These countries signed a document asking Egypt to negotiate without their making any specific demands regarding the fate of the hijackers in the event of their surrender.'

These varying statements reveal how deeply embarrassed both Italy and Egypt were from the political point of view and how keenly they felt the need to justify, one way or another, a diplomatic move that did entail many advantages (which I shall go into later), but which was rather too hasty, resulting as it did from highly dramatic circumstances, surrounded by 'shadows' which later proved difficult to explain away.

THE AGREEMENT'S MERITS

From a diplomatic, political and even psychological point of view, the agreement to give the hijackers a safe conduct was in many respects a success. First, it put an end to the hijacking, without giving in to the terrorists' demands that Israel release 50 Palestinians from prison: demands which could never have been met in any case. The terrorists seemed quite prepared to give in, being content with the relative 'success' of their operation. They had succeeded in drawing the attention of the world to the imprisonment of Palestinian freedom fighters in Israeli gaols; the hijackers also seemed pleased that the PLO should have been the counterpart in international negotiations with sovereign states (Egypt and Italy). Second, under the implicit terms of the agreement, the hijacking was to end without any loss of life (although this is not how things eventually turned out; I shall return to this point later). Here the advantage was obvious: to have persuaded the four Palestinians to abandon the hijacking was an enormous coup, both because so many innocent lives had been saved and because, had the hijacking gone on any longer, unpredictable international consequences could have ensued (such as an armed attack by the United States on the *Achille Lauro*, which – as Ambassador Rabb had hinted to Craxi – was a possibility). From this point of view the agreement for safe conduct had thrown a bucket of water on a fuse that was just about to ignite a huge powder keg.

A third, quite considerable, advantage was that the agreement did not declare formally that the hijackers should get off scot free: they were to be handed over to the PLO, and Arafat had already stated that he would have them tried and, if they were found guilty of any offences, punished. And indeed, Article 162 of the 1979 'Revolutionary Penal Code' of the PLO provides for the imprisonment of Palestinians who, *inter alia*, carry out hijackings of vessels belonging to 'friendly or foreign states'. Thus, the document did not endorse an act of terrorism, because the terrorists were expected to be tried and, eventually, punished.

A fourth 'useful' feature of the agreement was that it gave the PLO greater legitimacy as an international actor. The PLO was not one of the parties to the agreement. On a purely formal plane, it had been concluded by sovereign states and only they were bound to respect it. However, whereas the hijackers were the direct *beneficiaries* of the agreement (because in the event they were able to 'extricate themselves' without being tried or punished), the PLO found itself in a very similar position to that of the contracting states. Its representatives had taken part in the negotiations, and the agreement would never have been reached without their contribution and consent. Besides, the PLO did 'benefit' from the agreement, because it implicitly granted that organization the right (and also, perhaps, the duty) to try and eventually punish the hijackers.

From the legal point of view, it is debatable whether this 'benefit' to the PLO went so far as to give it the right to demand respect for the agreement from Egypt and Italy. Under international law an agreement between two or more states may contain clauses intended to benefit a third state. If the latter explicitly or tacitly agrees to those clauses, it acquires the right to insist that the contracting states respect them. Doubts on this point arise from the fact that not all three contracting states have recognized the PLO as an international subject (the Federal Republic of Germany, in particular, has not even granted it *de facto* recognition). Further, it is impossible to tell from the very succinct text of the agreement whether the three states intended to presuppose the international personality of the PLO.

However, this formal issue seems to be of quite secondary

importance. Clearly, the leaders of the PLO never took into serious consideration the issue of the organization's legal personality. Far more important from their point of view was the *political legitimacy* they had achieved by the agreement and by their being treated as fully-fledged international actors. The fact that the hijackers were to be handed over to the PLO and that Arafat had promised to have them tried by the Organization meant that the PLO was placed almost on a par with a sovereign state, with all the prerogatives of a body governing by means of an executive and a judiciary. And yet it is worth noting – despite Arafat's affirmations on the matter, later reiterated in more brazen terms by Abul Abbas – that on 10 October the PLO 'Foreign Minister', Farouk Kaddoumi, declared in New York that the hijackers would have to be tried jointly by the PLO, Egypt and Italy, since the Organization had 'no territory' wherein the hijackers might face a criminal trial.

THE AGREEMENT'S AMBIGUITIES

Although the agreement undoubtedly had its strong points, this is no reason to pass over a shadowy or equivocal area that weakened its effect and caused Egypt (and, at least initially, Italy too) to adopt an ambiguous attitude.

As I have already said, according to some of the actors in this drama, the agreement was reached on the understanding that the hijackers had not murdered anyone on board the *Achille Lauro*. But this 'understanding' was never explicitly spelled out in the text of the agreement, as it should have been, given the persistent rumours – supported by the hijackers' own declarations over the radio – that at least two hostages had been killed.

Why then did the parties not insist on including such a condition in the actual text of the agreement? Perhaps they did not do so because they decided that it was not politically expedient; and that it would serve their interests to act somewhat hypocritically. Indeed, in an interview on 11 October the Italian ambassador to Cairo, Mr G. Migliuolo, spoke revealingly of the 'hocus-pocus' or trick that had been played in omitting any mention of the 'condition' from the agreement. It was more than likely that the crimes had been committed. If they had been mentioned explicitly as a 'condition', this might have incurred two risks. First, by voicing their suspicions in a formal document, they would have cast the hijackers in a bad light, thereby running the risk of putting the PLO 'off-side'. Secondly, if their suspicions were correct, the agreement would have been null and void and the negotiators would have found themselves back at square one, with hundreds of hostages still in the hands of the Palestinians. Furthermore, one should not forget that during the negotiations in Cairo, the Americans were still impressing upon the Italian Government the need to use force and 'threatening' to send their commandos to board the *Achille Lauro*. Any clause that introduced even a tiny gap into the arrangement which was being negotiated could have brought about its collapse, thereby blocking the way for further negotiations and leaving room for military violence by either side.

EGYPT'S ATTITUDE AFTER THE AGREEMENT

The ambiguities of the safe-conduct agreement explain, in part, Egypt's actions *after* it had been entered into. For example, it explains why, once the terrorists had gone ashore (early afternoon of 10 October) and Captain De Rosa had told the Italian Government (in the late afternoon of the same day) that at least one passenger had been killed, officials of the Egyptian Government *turned a deaf ear and continued to consider the agreement valid*, allowing the hijackers and Abul Abbas to board an Egyptian plane and take off for Tunis (see above, chapter 3).

Before I try to discover the reasons for this strange pretence, I should like to highlight another contradiction in the attitude of the Egyptians. *At the very moment and immediately after* they had 'taken charge' of the four hijackers, the Egyptians stated that there was no indication of a murder having been committed; yet, a couple of weeks later, President Mubarak changed his version of the facts. In an interview with *Time* (25 October 1985), he made some revealing statements. On being asked when he had heard of Klinghoffer's death and why he had not handed over the hijackers, Mubarak replied: 'Nearly at midnight [9 October] we heard that an American man had been killed. So I decided, instead of freeing these people, I would send them to a country where a responsible representative of the PLO would take them. In one of his statements Arafat said, "If we receive them, we are going to put these people on trial." Then President Reagan agreed to that [in a statement made in Chicago on 9 October]. He changed his mind for one reason or another. But anyway it seemed convenient to send these people to the PLO as a test for Arafat. We had no right to put them on trial here. That of course would create lots of problems in our country politically. Secondly, I wanted to avoid more violence and retaliation against the Italians and Americans. And my experience said that violence will lead to more violence. That is why I preferred to send them to Arafat.'

One cannot expect a top-ranking politician to know the law and apply it, whatever the political costs. But this declaration is indeed astonishing because it completely contradicts the previous statements of Egyptian officials; moreover, it *totally* ignores the safe-conduct agreement, as well as another treaty binding Egypt (the 1979 Convention on the Taking of Hostages), which I shall discuss later on. The only conclusion we can draw from Mubarak's declaration is that respect for the law (whether international or domestic) never entered into his decisions, which were dictated solely by political considerations.

Let us now return to the statements made by various

CANISIUS COLLEGE LIBRARY
BUFFALO, N. Y.

Egyptian officials when the hijackers left Cairo, or immediately thereafter. By analysing these statements, as well as the political and diplomatic stance of Egypt during the affair, I hope to reveal the political motives underlying the decisions taken in Cairo and also to throw some light on Mubarak's interview with *Time*.

Egypt found itself in an awkward position, not only from the political and diplomatic points of view, but because of legal 'complications' as well. Together with the United States and the Federal Republic of Germany, Egypt was a party to the 1979 Convention on the Taking of Hostages. Italy was not at the relevant time a party; having signed it in 1980 and ratified it only in 1986. Article 5 of the Convention required Egypt either to *try* the hijackers or to *extradite* them to the United States (since numerous passengers on board the *Achille Lauro*, including Klinghoffer, were US citizens). The American Ambassador to Cairo had not initialled the agreement precisely because it derogated from this article in the Convention. Without American consent the agreement was not binding on the United States, and so Egypt was still under an obligation to respect the dictates of the Convention.

I should add that the Federal Republic of Germany was in a very different position. Like the United States, it had already ratified the 1979 Convention. By signing the safe-conduct agreement, Germany agreed to derogate from the Convention in the case of the *Achille Lauro* affair (and only *vis–à–vis* Egypt; as far as the United States was concerned, the FRG was still bound by the Convention). In other words, the Convention did not apply to the hijackers of the Italian liner in so far as the bilateral relations of Egypt and the Federal Republic of Germany were concerned.

As regards the United States, Egypt was bound to try the hijackers – unless it wanted to hand them over to the Americans – for having taken hostages, irrespective of whether or not any other crimes had been committed on board the *Achille Lauro*. Indeed, as far as the United States was concerned, the safe-conduct agreement was not legally relevant:

in legal terms it was *res inter alios acta* (an act performed by others and valid only for them).

Obviously, Egypt was on the horns of dilemma. It could *respect* its commitments *vis-à-vis* the USA (and other states that had ratified the 1979 Convention). But then Egypt ran the risk of terrorist reprisals from Abul Abbas' group and a worsening of its political relations with the PLO (only one year after these relations had improved). Moreover, conditions at home made such a solution undesirable: pro–Palestinian factions inside Egypt, which had long criticized Mubarak for being pro–American and had urged him to do more for Arafat, would certainly have fomented dangerous political tension in the country. Political instability was rife at that time and the Mubarak Government was already fairly precarious. The only alternative was to *ignore* the legal dictates of the 1979 Convention, in the hope that the United States would not react too heavy-handedly.

By not trying the hijackers or handing them over to the Americans (who, it appears, did not actually request their extradition), Egypt was guilty, from a technical point of view, of having disregarded its obligations towards the United States. Why then did it *pretend* it knew nothing about, or did not believe in, the murder of Klinghoffer? To what purpose? It gained no *legal* advantage thereby. However, from the *political and diplomatic* point of view the advantage was obvious: Egypt was respecting an agreement with two of the United States' allies (one also a party to the 1979 Convention, which in this case Egypt had chosen not to respect). By insisting that it had to adhere to the safe-conduct agreement, Egypt *legitimized* its behaviour on a *political* plane. Although it was violating a treaty with the USA (and other states), it was doing so only so as to be able to respect another agreement with two other Western nations. Respect for that agreement mitigated, to some extent, its violation of the 1979 Convention. Indeed, the promise to deliver the hijackers to the PLO, after Arafat had asked to try them himself, tinged Egyptian behaviour with a veneer of respect for the 1979 Convention (which specified – as I have pointed out before – that those who apprehend hostage-takers must either punish or extradite them).

On a cost–gains ratio, Egypt felt it was less expensive both politically and diplomatically to violate the 1979 treaty than to provoke a rupture in its relations with the Palestinians, quite apart from the repercussions this might have had on internal affairs. I do not intend to appraise here whether their decision to disregard a formal duty, undertaken years earlier with the United States, did in fact prove beneficial to Egypt on the political and diplomatic planes. Admittedly, such decisions are sometimes justified by the need to avoid an international or domestic backlash, especially if this might precipitate a serious crisis and endanger many lives. Strict respect for international law may, in other words, be waived if it is outweighed by grave danger to peace and to human lives. In my view, rules of international law should never be ignored, however, when their aim is to preserve peace and security or respect for human dignity, not to mention the prevention of an international crisis.

One might object that, in the *Achille Lauro* affair, by not observing the 1979 Convention, and by its 'legal fictions' and other practical dodges, Egypt ran a serious risk: if the PLO failed to punish the hijackers and their leaders, Klinghoffer's murder would go unpunished. By transgressing the law, Egypt almost blocked the path of justice. To this objection one might reply that if one had to choose between omitting to punish the murderers and the instigators on the one hand, and averting a serious crisis for both Egypt and the international community on the other, then the balance would be likely to swing in favour of the latter.

The alternatives, as you can judge for yourselves, are equally serious. No one has a right to determine which should have prevailed; though, in private, we may each form our own view as to the better choice.

5

The Attitude of
the American Government

By 1985 when the *Achille Lauro* was hijacked, the United States had formulated a complex 'doctrine' in relation to terrorist attacks on American 'objectives' abroad. It was quite obvious that the hijacking did not catch the United States unprepared. There are two reasons for this. The first is that a superpower with strategic, economic and political interests in every corner of the globe and with citizens and state agencies almost everywhere, cannot but carefully plan its actions by anticipating the possible strategy, behaviour and operations of other international subjects (states and non-state organizations). The second, more specific reason is that whereas the United States had hardly suffered any terrorist attacks on its own territory, abroad it had become the terrorists' favourite target, for political and historical reasons that we all know.

Let me just mention a few of the most serious of these 'episodes' in the Middle East prior to the *Achille Lauro* hijacking. In 1983 one of the Marines' barracks in Lebanon was blown up by Hezbollah groups (apparently financed and inspired by Iran), killing a large number of American soldiers; towards the end of 1984 a bomb went off in one of the American Embassy buildings in Beirut, also resulting in a great number of casualties; in 1985 various US citizens were kidnapped in Lebanon by terrorist groups; on 13 June of that same year, a TWA aircraft was hijacked as it flew from Athens to Beirut (one American was killed and others held hostage for a number of days). These were some of the most sinister terrorist attacks in a restricted geographical area (admittedly the worst 'hot spot' for Americans in the 1980s). It has been calculated that between 1980 and 1984 there were roughly 860 terrorist attacks in the Middle East, Latin America and Western Europe on American officials, citizens or property.

What are the cornerstones of the US 'strategy'? They can easily be extracted from the declarations of various high-ranking Americans, such as that of the Secretary of State, George Shultz, on 4 February 1985, or that of his Legal Adviser, Judge Sofaer, on 15 July that same year. In a nutshell, American strategy hinges on four main points. First, no compromise should ever be reached with terrorists and none of their demands should ever be met (although, in some cases, it can be useful to keep in touch with terrorist organizations in order to secure the release of hostages taken, without giving in to the terrorists' demands). Secondly, 'maximum diplomatic pressure' should be applied on states either directly, or indirectly, involved in acts of terrorism. Thirdly, if a policy of firmness does not bring about a solution to the crisis, the only possible alternative is to use armed force against the state that is financing, supporting or directing the terrorists, or – if hostages have been taken – in the state that shows itself unable to save the lives of the hostages, even though it may not itself be responsible for the act of terrorism. Fourthly, in the long run any solution to the problem of terrorism depends on international cooperation: international legal instruments must be set up, in the form of multilateral treaties; economic and political sanctions should be adopted against states that organize or shelter terrorist groups; finally, police and intelligence action throughout the western world must be coordinated.

This is obviously an essentially *repressive* strategy. As a long-term policy, the repression of the terrorist phenomenon can be achieved by coordinating the action of all democratic states (identifying and 'neutralizing' terrorist groups, forestalling their attacks and arresting those responsible for terrorist offences). In the short term (that is, in a crisis) the stolid intransigence of the Americans leaves them no alternative but to use force. There is no trace anywhere in these declarations, or in others made in recent years, of an understanding of the need to remove the social, economic and political causes of terrorism.

THE LEGAL GROUNDS ADDUCED BY THE UNITED STATES FOR USING FORCE AGAINST TERRORISTS

Within this general framework, how do the Americans justify *the use of force* against terrorists? On a formal, or legal, plane, one is referred to the idea of self-defence, as it is embodied in Article 51 of the UN Charter, one of the mainstays of that impressive organization set up in San Francisco in June 1945. As I mentioned earlier, the Americans believe they have a right to use force in self-defence in two circumstances: first, when the lives of American nationals are threatened because they have been kidnapped or taken prisoner by terrorists, and the authorities of the state where they are being held either cannot, or will not, do anything to set them free; secondly, in response either to a single outrageous terrorist attack organized and carried out by a state (using 'unofficial' terrorist groups to act for it), or else to a series of attacks which, taken singly, may not be so serious, but taken together cause considerable damage to American possessions, nationals or officials. As an example of the first, think of Israel's attack on Palestinian terrorists in 1975, at Entebbe airport in Uganda – considered an archetype for this kind of self-defence. Another instance was America's abortive attempt to free the US hostages held in Iran in 1980. The second class is best exemplified by the United States' attack on Libyan military bases on 15 April 1986, provoked by the bomb outrage in West Berlin (which, the Americans claimed, had been organized by terrorists acting under orders from Qaddafi).

However, many acts of terrorism cannot be neatly fitted into one of these two pigeon-holes. For example, if the intelligence services of one country discover that a ship or aircraft of another state is transporting terrorists that have just committed some outrage or are about to do so, can that country intercept and stop the ship or plane, in order to arrest the terrorists? By no stretch of the imagination can such a case be equated with the two 'classical' ones I described above. Here force would be used against a ship or plane belonging to a state that has nothing to do with terrorism, or, at least, is in no way responsible for the acts of the terrorist group. What should a state do in such circumstances? Does US 'strategy' provide for such a case and, if so, how?

The only episode that can throw some light on the United States' attitude, before the *Achille Lauro* hijacking, goes back to 1973. On 10 August of that year a Caravelle belonging to Middle East Airlines, on charter to Iraqi Airways, was intercepted by two Israeli fighter planes after it had left Beirut airport and was heading for Baghdad. This civilian airliner was forced to land in an Israeli military base; all 83 passengers were then ordered to disembark, together with the seven members of the crew, and were questioned for many hours. The Israelis apparently thought that there were a number of terrorists aboard. Once the Israeli military were certain their information was incorrect, the aircraft was allowed to depart. The very next day the UN Security Council was urgently convened. Israel justified its action by saying that it had acted in self-defence: it had merely exercised its right to use force to protect its nationals from terrorist attacks. But all the members of the Security Council, including the United States, disagreed and, in the end, unanimously adopted a resolution severely condemning Israel.

In view of the United States' attitude when other aircraft were later intercepted, in 1985 and 1986, I feel it is well worth examining the US delegate's important statements and highlighting the main points. Before the resolution condemning Israel was adopted, but after that state had justified its action

by referring to the principle of self-defence, the US delegate
made the following statement:

There can be no doubt that such actions by their very nature place
the lives of the innocent persons aboard an aircraft in danger. . . .We
[the United States] deplore this violation of the United Nations
Charter and of the rule of law in international civil aviation.
Fortunately, no lives were lost and no material damage was incurred
in this latest incident. While this does not modify our concern, we
strongly urge all parties to retain a sense of perspective and prevent
this incident from leading to further reprisals and counter-reprisals.
It is high time to call a halt to all such acts and related acts and
threats of violence. The representative of Israel has explained that
the purpose of his Government's action in diverting the airliner
was to apprehend individuals responsible for terrorist acts. My
Government has been second to none in its condemnation of
international terrorism, in the search for new instruments of
international law to counter terrorism, and in urging other Governments to take a strong stand and adopt effective measures against
those who endanger and take innocent lives in the name of serving
a political cause. National and international efforts to control
terrorism must go forward. *They must, however, go forward within
and not outside the law.* The commitment to *the rule of law* in
international affairs, including the field of international civil
aviation, *imposes certain restraints on the methods* Governments can use
to protect themselves against those who operate outside the law. My
Government believes actions such as Israel's diversion of a civil
airliner on 10 August *are unjustified* and likely to bring about counter-
action on an increasing scale. (Emphasis added)

It is indeed hard to imagine a more explicit or better reasoned
condemnation of Israel's action. Yet, after the resolution had
been passed by the Security Council, the US delegate went
further. In his comments on the resolution he made some
remarks that should be remembered for the value they acquire
ex post (and we shall shortly see why). He said:

The fact that this resolution confines itself to expressing the
Council's condemnation of a specific incident should serve as no

comfort to anyone contemplating illegal acts of violence or terrorism. Rather, it is *a warning to all members of the world community* that the community *will no longer tolerate illegal interference with one of the basic means of communication from any quarter.* Should there be further instances of *international lawlessness* or terror, I most sincerely hope that this body will again demonstrate similar unity and determination. Nor should our vote be read to mean any commitment to any kind of specific measures. Terrorism, illegal violence and threats to the innocent must stop. Humanity depends on it; our conscience demands it. We, for our part, *will continue to oppose such actions whether by Governments, individuals or groups, regardless of nationality or of motivation.* (Emphasis added)

In the light of this precedent and of the stance adopted by the United States, it would appear that the American Administration believed that terrorism could be fought militarily only in the two cases I mentioned earlier, but that force could not be used in a case such as the one I have just referred to. Later on we shall see how faithful the United States has been to the policy advocated in 1973.

POLITICS AND DIPLOMACY:
US ATTITUDES IN THE *ACHILLE LAURO* AFFAIR

The overall picture of events I have tried to paint in the preceding pages may now serve as a background to American behaviour in the affair. In some ways, after the Italian liner had been hijacked, the Americans acted in a manner perfectly consistent with US 'strategy'. If anything, America reduced its room for political and diplomatic manoeuvre still further: from the very beginning, the Americans chose a line of complete intransigence, showing a determination not to negotiate, since, in their view, only the use of force could solve the crisis.

President Reagan immediately stated that he was opposed to any form of negotiation with the terrorists and this emerges quite clearly not only from the declarations of the White

House on 9 and 10 October 1985, but also from what Craxi said in his speech on 17 October about the American stance. When, on Monday 7 October, the Americans requested Italy to 'ask Arafat to announce publicly that he had no part in the act of terrorism', this was obviously not a sign that they were prepared to cooperate with the hijackers, but merely that they wished to ascertain where the latter stood politically, the better to isolate them.

Apart from this apparent sign of flexibility, the American Government – as Craxi said in his speech – showed itself 'completely averse to taking part in any form of negotiation'. Its refusal to negotiate emerged both when the Syrians asked the United States and the United Kingdom if they were prepared to accept Syrian mediation, and in subsequent declarations (from Tuesday 8 October on, by the Defence Secretary, Caspar W. Weinberger, amongst others) to the effect that the government in Washington was ready to 'initiate military action' (as Rabb had told Craxi, see chapter 3). American intransigence was also evident in that country's dealings with Egypt, after the latter had helped the hijackers to disembark. It reached a climax when the Egyptian aircraft was intercepted, not to mention the 'tug-of-war' with the Italian military at Sigonella and the later violation by American jet fighters of Italian air space (between Sigonella and Ciampino, and again at Ciampino).

This leads us to ask *three quesions*. First, what were the political and diplomatic reasons that made the Americans adopt such an intransigent line? Secondly, how did they justify their most flagrant and controversial action, the interception of the Egyptian Boeing, and what political and diplomatic consequences did this interception entail? Thirdly, did suitable and practical alternatives to the use of armed force exist?

As for the first question, I believe that there were three reasons for the United States' being 'completely averse to taking part in any form of negotiation'. The first was the need to be consistent with the Washington 'doctrine' on terrorism.

The second was a natural consequence of Klinghoffer's murder: American public opinion – which had already been irritated by previous examples of governmental 'impotence' – then became so incensed that Reagan felt that he must make some flamboyant gesture and prove to the man in the street that a superpower will not allow a group of terrorists to murder its citizens and get away with it. In this he was right: the hijacking of the Boeing was greeted with jubilation 'back home' and one of Reagan's staff even went so far as to describe this as a 'God-sent opportunity' for raising national morale. The third reason for the American intransigence was its effect abroad. The whole world – especially states that support, abet or condone terrorist organizations, as well as states which (like Egypt) feel obliged in special circumstances not to use their anti-terrorist powers to a full extent – was meant to take note. A superpower, such as the United States, is not, and never will be, shackled by international rules of behaviour or ties of friendship or good diplomatic relations when it has to save defenceless Americans, or punish terrorists who endanger their lives. Thus, the use of force against the Egyptian airliner acquired a meaning that transcended the whole affair and served as a future warning to the world.

LEGAL 'GROUNDS' FOR INTERCEPTING THE EGYPTIAN AIRLINER

Is it a futile question?

How did the Americans try to justify their interception of the Egyptian plane? The answer to this question is bound to be extremely complex. The more sceptical reader (and perhaps there are many), who regards international law with a jaundiced eye, may feel that the question itself is useless. What point is there in asking how the Americans tried to find legal grounds to justify their behaviour, since, even if there had not been any, their unlawful action would still have gone 'unpunished'? The UN Security Council (the only body that could have issued a condemnation) is only capable of 'paper' condemnations and even these are subject to veto by each of the permanent members (including the United States). I do not agree, however, that the question is pointless: I feel it is well worth answering. The United States, unlike so many other nations, firmly believes in the rule of law. The concept is deeply rooted in the American system and in US history and culture; its effects are felt even in US foreign policy. As Judge Sofaer put it recently: 'Americans are particularly attracted to the law as a means for repressing violence, and are committed domestically and internationally to using law to control criminal conduct and to resolve disputes. They invoke the law almost instinctively, and repeatedly, assuming that it regulates international conduct and, in particular, provides a system for bringing terrorists to justice.' Without a doubt, the United States is one of the few countries in which the most important acts of foreign policy are reviewed in the light of international law by the State Department. (Indeed, the compilations of legal documentation concerning American foreign relations are far more substantial than those existing in other states. Furthermore, the Legal Adviser to the Secretary of State has much more influence than his counterpart elsewhere. This being so, there is a valid reason for inquiring into American attitudes during the *Achille Lauro* affair. Did the United States regard itself as following the dictates of international law? Or, considering or declaring that vital interests were at stake, did it consciously decide to ignore the law, doing so either openly and explicitly, or in a roundabout way, by 'manipulating' the rules?

After inquiring into how the United States judged itself and how it explained its actions in the light of international law, one should pose the same question from an objective, non–American point of view (to the extent that this is possible): how far did American conduct conform with the rules of the international community? In my view such a question is legitimate; after all, the international community does not follow maxims that govern the conduct of domestic affairs, according to which – as Pascal noted – justice changes with latitude and what is true on one side of the Pyrenees is false on the other. A consensus has now formed on a set of rules to regulate relations between states; these rules enshrine values and interests that all states, or almost all, hold dear. In principle at least, Good and Evil should not vary according to latitude and longitude. It is therefore pertinent to ask whether or not, in a case such as the *Achille Lauro* incident, a superpower has respected these rules and why. On a practical plane, of course, the answer will be of no use, at least in the short term. However, it will serve to widen our understanding of international affairs, including the motives behind a state's actions, as well as our knowledge of whether these rules contain any loopholes. In the long run an answer can also serve a further purpose: by criticizing and denouncing deviant behaviour we may, in time, be able to help reduce anarchy in the international community.

Applicable international rules

Before we begin to examine the Americans' position in detail, it may prove useful to remind the reader which international rules were applicable to our case according both to state practice and to the bulk of legal literature.

When, in 1945, states met in San Francisco to lay the foundations for a new world organization, they made a solemn promise: they would banish from international relations not only the use of force, but the mere threat to use force. As they were just emerging from the devastating effects of a world war, they hoped to build a dyke against future horrors. This solemn pact was embodied in Article 2, paragraph 4, of the United Nations Charter. The article was intended as *a point of no return* in the life of the international community. After centuries of conflict and the death and misery left behind by war, for the first time in history, the mighty had met to erect not only a legal barrier, but an institutional fortress against the unleashing of future violence. The ideas that inspired Kant and the Age of Enlightenment seemed to have come to life, and reason seemed to have prevailed over the darker side of human nature. Unlike so many legal rules, which seem to be written in invisible ink (requiring a jurist's potion to make them visible and his oracular skills to make them comprehensible), Article 2, paragraph 4, is quite simple and clear in its meaning. Anyone, from the civil servant concerned with domestic matters to the diplomat, from the soldier to the man in the street, can immediately understand it. Had this not been so, the states convened in San Francisco would have made only a 'verbal' pledge, one that would have been forgotten the moment a new international crisis blew up.

One point deserves special emphasis. Article 2, paragraph 4, not only bans war and the threat of war: it also bans the *use of lesser kinds of violence*. Take for example, the resort to armed reprisals (a violent reaction to the unlawful behaviour of others). Just such an episode involved Italy, on 31 August 1923, when Mussolini had Corfu bombarded as a reprisal for alleged Greek complicity in the killing of General Tellini and some of his men by terrorists. Article 2, paragraph 4 was intended to banish violence in *any form whatsoever*. It achieved this aim by branding as unlawful all violence in international relations, but also by establishing a framework of guarantees against future breaches of the rule.

However, states felt that there should be an exception to the ban on the use of force. They feared, quite rightly, that the enforcement mechanism set up in San Francisco (to arm the ban with a 'sword') might become jammed. Moreover, they wanted to provide for exceptional circumstances when, even if the mechanism were working, instant action was necessary before the UN forces could be martialled against the aggressor. This exception was the famous Article 51 on self-defence: every state has a right to use force to *repulse an armed attack* by another state, until the Security Council has a chance to intervene. I have already described, in another book (*Law and Violence in the Modern Age*, 1988), how this exception was, in time, expanded by states to such an extent that it now includes two categories of the use of force that were not foreseen in 1945. These are the use of force to protect one's nationals abroad (when they are threatened by great and imminent danger), and the so-called anticipatory self-defence, or use of force, not to repel an actual attack, but to prevent it from taking place (provided, of course, the danger of this aggression is very real and imminent; it threatens the very life of the defending state; and it cannot be avoided otherwise).

Now, Article 2, paragraph 4, and Article 51 are the parallels between which states may move in deciding whether to resort to armed force. Many states say they will respect these limits, and actually do so. This applies – to some extent – to the United States. In some respects, American anti-terrorist 'strategy' is fenced in by the two Articles: it allows the use of force to save the lives of US citizens threatened by terrorist groups in states that either cannot or will not do anything to protect those citizens, or against states that organize and direct terrorist attacks.

US embarrassment

Before we scrutinize American justifications, I should like to explain just how useful the concepts contained in the previous paragraphs are in revealing the exact contours of American behaviour. The Americans certainly could not appeal to the concept of *armed reprisal* to justify their interception of the Egyptian aircraft; in other words, they could not claim to have used force in response to an unlawful act by Egypt (its breach of the 1979 Convention on the Taking of Hostages). If the unlawful act of a state does not take the form of an armed attack (Egypt's attempt to hand the hijackers over to the PLO could in no way be seen as an armed attack), then the state which is the victim of the unlawful act cannot react by using force. Article 2, paragraph 4, is explicit on this point.

Nor could the Americans claim the right to *self-defence*. To do so they would have to show that the state against which they used force was also the state that was endangering the lives of the hostages (whereas in fact the hostages on board the *Achille Lauro* had already been set free), or that that state had used armed force or was about to do so (Egypt had neither used force against the US passengers, nor was it intending to do so; indeed, it was making every possible effort to achieve a peaceful solution to the crisis, thus doing its utmost to help all passengers, including the Americans).

Since neither ground could be advanced by the United States to justify its use of force against the Egyptian Boeing, it is easy to understand that nation's embarrassment *after* the interception. One is struck by the American Government's uneasiness and reticence on the subject. In this case, the State Department has never adduced legal grounds for the action; it has merely dropped (deliberately?) *vague hints*. Others (such as President Reagan and the Judge of the Court in the District of Columbia who signed the warrant for Abul Abbas' provisional arrest) have also given some indications on this subject; but again their justifications are implicit and not very detailed and, to a certain extent, contradict what was stated by the State Department. Whereas President Reagan and the judge claim that the hijackers were *pirates* and this in itself, they imply, would justify the Americans' use of force, the State Department hints that the hijackers were a *kind of modern incarnation of the pirates of former times*; if one *equates* them with pirates, then one can deal with them as if they were indeed pirates.

Let me add that, in my opinion, there were only *two* real attempts at justifying the incident, because what Defence Secretary Weinberger said, on 11 October 1985, can hardly be taken as a justification. He merely stated: 'international law offered a solid basis for adopting this [military] course.' On being asked what this basis was, he had nothing to add. Nor can we accept as a justification the surprisingly naive statement made by the Secretary of the Navy, John F. Lehman Jr, in an interview on 13 October 1985 (in answer to the question on the Egyptians' objection to the interception of their airliner): 'It is like a murderer hailing a taxi, and then the taxi company pretending they were the target of the police arrest. The fact is, the pirates in the airplane were the target of the intercept, and they happened to be in a civilian Egyptian airliner.' Obviously, the Secretary did not appreciate the difference between a taxi and the aircraft of a sovereign state!

I hope what I say in the next few pages will convince my readers that it is well worth examining the various theses the Americans advanced as justification.

The hijackers as pirates

Both Reagan and the judge who signed the warrant for Abul Abbas' provisional arrest characterized the hijackers as pirates. This idea was upheld later by two American commentators (P. S. Edelman and G. P. McGinley) in legal journals. What was implied by this? It meant that any state could arrest them and try them for their piracy, just as if they had been buccaneers from the Caribbean over two hundred years ago. Therefore, like any other state, the United States had every right to capture the hijackers and bring them to justice; consequently, their interception of the Egyptian airliner was quite legitimate. Although this theory was mentioned *en passant* by Reagan, it figured quite explicitly in the 'reasons' given for the warrant for Abul Abbas' provisional arrest and in the articles by the two American commentators mentioned above. It is hardly surprising that Reagan did not insist too forcefully on the hijackers being pirates, as the theory is quite groundless (and indeed, Sofaer did not reiterate it in his subsequent statement).

The pirates with which international law is concerned are those described in the books of Defoe, Stevenson and Voltaire, and have existed since Roman times. (The famous phrase describing pirates as the 'enemies of all mankind' comes from Cicero: *communis hostis omnium.*) Their period of greatest prominence was in the seventeenth and eighteenth centuries, but they gradually disappeared after that time and the new technological age has almost eliminated them completely: they were unable to cope with warships powered by steam and the use of the telegraph. These pirates were men who threatened the freedom of the high seas, by boarding ships to rob them. International law does allow any state to act against pirates, but only on three conditions: first, the attack must take place on the high seas; secondly, the pirates must board the merchant ship from their own vessel; thirdly, the purpose of their action must be to seize merchandise they find on the ship they assault; in other words, they must act 'for private ends'. Only under these conditions does international law allow *any state throughout the world* – hence, even a state that has no citizens on board the assaulted vessel – to stop the pirate ship by force, arrest the pirates, try them and hang them (if need be).

In the *Achille Lauro* incident – quite apart from the problem of exactly *where* the liner was when it was hijacked, as well as the fact that the four Palestinians were *already on board* the ship they attacked – the terrorists certainly did not hijack the ship for 'private ends'. Their motivations, however execrable, were not 'private', but political. Thus, the hijackers could not be called pirates, in the classical sense of the term.

There is another objection to the piracy theory. Even assuming the four hijackers were pirates (and they were not), this did not legitimize the interception of the Egyptian airliner by US jet planes. International law allows states to attack the *pirates themselves*, or *their vessels*, not the ships or aircraft of sovereign states suspected of having pirates on board. A military ship or plane may exercise its 'right of visit' on board a ship in full sail, or a plane in flight, only if there is good reason to believe that it is *practising piracy*; this rule cannot apply to a ship or plane belonging to a sovereign state that is carrying (or suspected of carrying) 'pirates'.

The hijackers as 'modern pirates'

Before the airliner was intercepted, the Security Council was already discussing the difficult Middle Eastern question and the American delegate had outlined a justification that is worth examining. He pointed out that for centuries pirates have been considered the 'enemies of mankind', because they are a danger to shipping, human beings and goods. Terrorism, he suggested, is the modern equivalent to the piracy of former times: terrorists are 'the enemies of us all'.

The terrorist has put himself beyond the pale of civilized humanity. He should be shunned by all. If he seeks sanctuary he should be turned away. If he claims support he should be denounced. If he is apprehended he should be prosecuted. Every terrorist attack is an attack on the world community. Every justification offered for terrorism undermines the rule of law. Every concession to the terrorist diminishes our humanity.

It seems to me that his words and, to a certain extent, the statement made after the US interception of the Egyptian plane by President Reagan's deputy press secretary, reveal a fairly clear line of thought, though deliberately not a very explicit one: terrorism is the modern version of piracy; therefore, although the traditional preconditions for piracy do not apply to terrorism, all the powers attributed to states in their fight against pirates can also be used against terrorists. The United States acted in the interests of justice, to make sure that the authors of odious crimes, which offend the whole of mankind, were brought to court.

Unfortunately, this justification is also unacceptable. (Perhaps this is why the State Department never spelt it out in so many words, even though some American jurists, as well as the Legal Adviser to the State Department himself, have expressed the hope it would, sooner or later, be accepted into the fabric of international law.) Certainly, before the analogy between terrorists and pirates is admitted, it must clearly and explicitly be 'authorized' by the international community in the guise of a general rule. Although most countries express their strong condemnation of terrorism, such a general rule has not yet crystallized. It can only be said to have crystallized when there is sufficient evidence that it is accepted, and acted upon, by states as if it were law. Such a rule would obviously be another exception to Article 2, paragraph 4; it would thus stand beside the only other exception that is allowed at present: Article 51 of the UN Charter.

The second reason for rejecting the American theory is – as I said earlier – that the old rule on piracy *juris gentium* allowed states to use force against *specific individuals* (pirates) or against pirate vessels. In the *Achille Lauro* incident the United States used force against a state aircraft that was transporting the hijackers. If such an act was not allowed by the old international rule for real pirates, it could hardly become legitimate in the case of a hijacking. Thus, even if the analogy between terrorists and pirates were accepted, it would still not justify the American interception.

One last criticism of the American theory concerns the political and diplomatic implications of any future rule which authorizes force along the lines of the American action. It would lead us from our present state of semi-anarchy to one of total anarchy. The great powers, and the middle-sized ones too perhaps, would feel free to use force against foreigners – whom they chose to call 'terrorists' – wherever they might be. This would lead to increasing tension, and then conflict, between the 'enforcing states' and the states whose nationals these 'terrorists' were. Further, I believe it is important to remember that to accept the American theory would mean allowing the use of force not only against states that finance, organize and control terrorists (in which case these states would be responsible for the acts of terrorism), but also in very different circumstances, when a state is far less deeply involved, as in the case of Egypt during the *Achille Lauro* affair.

To get a clear picture of how much this theory would subvert the present system of law and order in the international community, one has only to remember instances in which states have acted violently against *individuals* living abroad. In such cases, the international community has consistently condemned the use of coercion against individuals without the prior consent of the local state, although admittedly this condemnation has been rather restrained in cases perceived as having some countervailing 'merit' (as in the case of the kidnapping of Eichmann by Israeli agents in Argentina). The (unauthorized) use of violence against *states* is condemned even more vigorously by the international community: nor does it make any difference whether violent acts are carried out on the territory of another state, on the high seas, or in international air space (the first differs from the other two instances because, not only is the *rule banning the use of force* violated, but also the *territorial sovereignty* of the other state is trampled underfoot).

FURTHER SHORTCOMINGS OF THE UNITED STATES' USE OF FORCE

The interception of the Egyptian aircraft as a 'precedent'

I have tried to show that the interception on 9–10 October was contrary to international law and that American justifications do not hold water. Later on I shall examine the political and diplomatic consequences this action had, in the short run, on relations with Egypt and Italy. Let us now take a look at one of the main errors of the interception: it has set a dangerous precedent, which other states may follow; indeed, one which has already been imitated. A few months after the incident, the Israelis took a leaf out of the Americans' book, thereby forcing the United States to endorse their action and to work out a new 'doctrine' on the intercepting of aircraft that has aroused the censure of most nations in the international community.

You may remember that, on 4 February 1986, a privately owned Libyan aircraft flying to Syria with an official delegation of Syrians on board was intercepted in international air space by two Israeli fighter planes and forced to land on Israeli territory. After checking all the passengers, and not finding any of the notorious terrorists they had expected to be there, the Israelis allowed the plane to depart. This was followed immediately by a heated debate in the Security Council where the United States essentially supported Israel, though with some reservations. The final resolution condemning Israel was blocked by an American veto; thus Israel escaped from the incident without even receiving a formal censure.

In the Security Council, before a vote on the resolution, Israel claimed that it had acted in self-defence pursuant to Article 51 of the UN Charter (see above). The Israeli representative was careful to stress that states, most notably Libya and Syria, were responsible for the terrorist activity against which Israel sought to protect itself. Outlining the history of terrorist activity against Israel, he said: 'Now this is not done by itself; there are people who perpetrate such actions. These people are assisted, indeed are launched, by Governments. Two of those Governments are involved in this case. One of them is Libya . . . the other is Syria.' And the delegate then proceeded to assert that the Syrian delegation was on its way to Libya to take part in a state-sponsored conference to discuss the organization of terrorist activities. Israeli intelligence had heard that the plane would have terrorists among its passengers, and this was why Israel had felt it necessary to use force against the aircraft. This was a case of 'self-defence', 'as it must be interpreted in the age of terrorism'. Thus, 'a nation attacked by terrorists is permitted to use force to prevent or pre-empt future attacks'; the Israeli delegate then went on to say that it is 'simply not serious to argue that international law prohibits us from capturing terrorists in international waters or international air space.'

A number of members of the Security Council explicitly rejected this theory. These included Algeria and Bulgaria (whose objections were echoed by the representative of the PLO); other states were implicitly critical of it (including some Third World countries and the socialist states, together with the United Kingdom, Australia, Denmark and France). Only the US delegate, while criticizing Israel on the facts, agreed with the Israeli interpretation of the law. It is worth examining the Americans' argument. General Walters (the US representative at the United Nations) stated as follows:

As a general principle the United States opposes the interception of civil aircraft. The safety of international aviation must be protected. . . . At the same time, we believe that there may arise exceptional circumstances in which an interception may be justified. As we have stated before in this forum, the United States recognizes and strongly supports the principle that a state whose territory or citizens are subjected to continuing terrorist attacks may respond with appropriate use of force to defend itself against further attacks. The appropriateness of a particular action will always raise considerations of necessity and proportionality. Where the target of a defensive action is an aircraft, heightened attention must be paid to considerations of safety. Because of the inherent risk involved in an action directed against an aircraft, such measures should be undertaken only in exceptional circumstances. The state taking action must meet a high burden of demonstrating that the particular decision was justified. The manner in which such an action is carried out is also significant. Even in a case where a state ultimately succeeds in apprehending a terrorist who constitutes a threat to its territory or citizens, the apprehending state must, in the course of its action, exercise every possible precaution, paying the greatest possible attention to the safety of the aircraft and those on board. A state's action to apprehend terrorists aboard an aircraft is a drastic measure not to be taken lightly. We believe a state should intercept a civilian aircraft only on the basis of the strongest and clearest evidence that terrorists are aboard. We do not believe that Israel has demonstrated that its action met this rigorous and necessary standard, and therefore we deplore that action. Nevertheless, because we believe that the ability to take such action in carefully defined and limited circumstances is an aspect of the inherent right of self-defence recognized in the United Nations Charter, my Government cannot accept a draft resolution [tabled by Congo, Ghana, Madagascar, Trinidad and Tobago and the United Arab Emirates, and aimed at condemning Israel] which implies that interception of an aircraft is wrongful *per se*, without regard to the possibility that the action may be justified. We can support no draft resolution that implicitly calls into question the exercise of this right.

Thus, only a few months after the Americans had used armed force against the Egyptian aircraft, the United States lost any sign of hesitation: whereas in October 1985 it had been felt that they could not present the theory as a formal justification, the Americans were now *proclaiming a 'doctrine' that introduced another dangerous loophole* into the exception to the ban on the use of force (Article 51). In fact, this 'doctrine' would justify coercive action against any civilian aircraft, so long as there was good reason to believe that it had terrorists aboard and providing every possible effort was made to avoid loss of life. In the end, despite his reservations, what the American representative was suggesting was acceptance of the notion that some states have the right to act as 'enforcers' of the law forbidding terrorism, with all the obvious risks that that would entail.

These risks were put, in very clear terms, by the delegate to the Security Council for the United Arab Emirates, Al-Shaali. I quote his words with great pleasure, because one rarely comes across so pertinent and convincing a speech (his words were directed exclusively against Israel's justification, because General Walters had not yet spoken). He said:

Allow me now to [make a] remark, an important one. The representative of Israel, in his first statement the day before yesterday, went beyond all the norms of international law. He gave a bizarre interpretation of the law when he arrogated to his country the right to intercept any civilian airliner if Israel believed some of the passengers on board were what he called terrorists or enemies of Israel. In addition to that being a violation of all international laws and conventions, in particular in 1944 Chicago Convention on Civil Aviation, which was modified on 10 May 1984, such an interpretation has another, more dangerous, meaning. It is that every state has the right to intercept any civilian airliner if it suspects there are on board terrorists or enemies of its Government. In the current international situation, very many examples could be given in this regard, without passing judgement on those I am about to mention. For instance, Japan would have the right to intercept any civilian airliner, whatever its nation of origin, if Japan believed members of the Red Army were on board that plane. Italy would have the right to intercept any aircraft if it believed members of the Red Brigade were on board. Britain would have the right to intercept any aircraft if it believed members of the IRA were on board. Nicaragua would have the right to intercept aircraft if it thought members of the *Contras* were on board. And so on. Every Government in the world has those it could consider to be terrorists or antagonists. Thus the world would be changed into a jungle in which hijacked aircraft and vessels would outnumber those flying or in transit. . . . Such a logic and such practices [by Israel], especially since they emanate from a state member of the United Nations, constitute a dangerous precedent that would consolidate land, sea and air piracy in the name of fighting terrorism. There is no doubt that such piratical logic jeopardizes civil aviation and transport on land and sea. Hence we must take the following facts into consideration. If we suppose, for the sake of argument – though we reject this supposition – there is justification for a certain state to hijack an aircraft because its intelligence service believes it has terrorists on board, what would happen to the aircraft and the innocent civilian passengers if the suspected terrorist blew up the aircraft or hijacked it from inside? . . . What would happen if the pilot refused to comply with the orders given him by the military jets, whether that was his own decision or resulted from a threat by one of the passengers on the plane?

These words are, I believe, a penetrating summary of the pernicious consequences of the American and Israeli 'legal doctrine'. It is hardly surprising, then, that his ideas were taken up, more or less explicitly, by the delegates from China, the USSR, Ghana, Algeria, Congo, as well as the United Kingdom.

The United States becomes irresolute and unsure of itself

The US action against the Egyptian aircraft had another unfortunate result: having had to find some kind of justification *after the event* for the interception and, later, being forced to approve the Israeli interception in 1986, the United States' legal attitude in such matters has become vacillating and contradictory. Whereas the Americans condemned the Israeli interception of the Iraqi plane (see above) in 1973, in 1985 the United States followed Israel's example, without giving any official justification for its action. A few months later, when Israel intercepted an Arab plane once again (in the confident belief that at least one superpower was not in a position to condemn its action this time), the Americans presented a formal justification for such an act that was totally inconsistent with what they had said in 1973. When a superpower – and one that is forever proclaiming its belief in the 'rule of law' and is continually asserting its desire to respect the legal standards governing the international community – bends those rules in specific circumstances to suit its purposes, it is clearly setting a very poor example to lesser powers.

One might object that the United States has merely *updated* its legal armoury to ward off the devastating effects of present-day terrorism, which in 1973 did not require states to react on such a large and dangerous scale. Today the cancerous effects of terrorism have spread throughout the body of the international community and states that suffer from its deadly attacks must react with exceptional measures. These measures – so the argument runs – should include the interception of foreign aircraft and ships suspected of carrying terrorists on board. It would be wrong to speak of inconsistency in the American approach to terrorism, because it is merely *adapting* its legal theories and its actions to an escalation in the frequency and danger of terrorist attacks.

No one would deny that terrorism has become ever more widespread, dangerous and transnational; it is also true that it poses a greater threat for some states than for others. However, this does not mean that a state – be it large or small – believing that it must find an answer to terrorist attacks, can *twist the rules as it pleases*. These rules reflect the practice and 'legal consciousness' of the world community. 'Reinterpretations' or adaptations of these rules which are not accepted by the majority of states are merely *unilateral manipulations* of them. In other words, General Walters' declaration (quoted above) is not a sign that the applicable rule of international law has changed. His words merely mean one state has taken a stance that runs counter to the prevailing law and has advanced a 'theory' which cannot but increase tension and dangers in the world community.

The short-term political and diplomatic consequences of the United States' use of force

So far I have outlined the long-term negative effects of the American action. However, in the short term it also had negative repercussions, though these could more easily be 'remedied'. It deeply offended Egypt, one of the United States' few friends in the Middle East, as well as causing a rift with its faithful ally, Italy.

By having one of their military planes fly over Italian territory (from Sigonella to Rome) without prior Italian authorization, the United States undoubtedly violated Italy's territorial sovereignty (hence Craxi's note of protest). It was an act of shameless arrogance and a sign of political ineptitude (why tail the Egyptian airliner, when an interception in Italian airspace was out of the question?). What reason was there for violating one of the most elementary international rules, unless the whole operation was the result of political incompetence, rather than a rational consideration of the alternatives to law-abiding behaviour?

However, what the Americans did to Egypt was far worse. Why humiliate a faithful friend (Mubarak spoke of being 'stabbed in the back'), a country which the United States is supporting on a massive scale, not only politically, but in the form of military and economic aid as well? (Egypt is second only to Israel on the list of nations that receive such aid from the United States.) One must not forget that Egypt is one of the pillars upholding western policy in the Middle East. For the sake of one act of violence, why destroy years of patient diplomatic effort that go back to before the Camp David agreements and which, since February 1985, had led to better relations between Egypt and Jordan? Above all, why deliver a slap in the face to a country that is undergoing a severe economic crisis and is in the grip of social, political and religious conflict, thereby endangering its political and institutional equilibrium?

It is hard to find rational answers to these questions. The administration may well have been aware of the negative effects of an interception, but decided to go ahead partly to assuage public opinion at home, and partly to send a signal of determination to the rest of the world (one, however, that could only have nefarious consequences, as I have just tried to show).

WERE THERE VALID ALTERNATIVES TO THE USE OF FORCE?

The American use of force against the Egyptian airliner was all the more deplorable since rational and peaceful alternatives that could have produced similar results did exist.

Prior to the interception the United States had already been told by Craxi that 'Italy intended to ask Egypt to extradite the four hijackers so that they could stand trial in Italy.' The Americans also knew that, if the hijackers were in the meantime transferred into the hands of the PLO, the Italian Government would ask that organization to extradite them: the Italian Foreign Minister was about to instruct the Italian Ambassador in Tunis to take the necessary steps to this end. (In his statement to the Chamber Craxi even stated that 'Arafat had already received a request to hand them over to Italy.')

In other words, the United States intercepted the Egyptian plane knowing that the appropriate steps had already been taken, or were about to be taken, to ensure that the hijackers would be arrested and tried. Worse still, the plane was intercepted while it was looking for a place to land (having been turned away by Tunisia and Greece) and, since it was an Egyptian aircraft, it would have flown home to Egypt (as I noted in chapter 3, the plane had indeed turned back to Cairo, according to a note from the Egyptian Foreign Ministry of 11 October 1985). Egypt had solemnly promised various states, including the USA, to punish or extradite anyone who had taken hostages. Admittedly, Cairo had already disregarded this duty. However, once the plane had landed on Egyptian soil, the Egyptian Government could no longer have pretended to know nothing of Klinghoffer's murder. Almost certainly, the gravity of this crime and the growing fury of public opinion, both in America and in other countries (including Italy), would have induced the Egyptians to abandon their policy of wheeling and dealing and made them face up to their legal duties. This would have given the United States an excellent card to play, without the need to trample the international rules of behaviour underfoot and without damaging the prestige of a Middle Eastern ally.

Thus, in this case international law did offer practical alternatives to the use of force: the hijackers could have been punished, either by Italy (as Craxi had assured Reagan he would do), or by Egypt (in accordance with the 1979 Convention, which was becoming increasingly difficult for Egypt to disregard).

Of course, one can object that Arafat was unlikely to hand over the hijackers to Italy. Arafat's reactions are always unpredictable. Would he have chosen to comply with the Italian extradition request, thereby giving his organization a new aura of international legitimacy, or would he have been swayed by the need to respond to internal pressure from Abul Abbas' group? Certainly, one cannot rule out that a solution based on respect for law might have been found, perhaps due to Tunisian mediation. In any case, when the airliner was intercepted *it had already been refused permission to land by Tunisia*. Therefore, the question of whether or not Arafat would in the event have upheld the rule of law is in the end irrelevant.

The United States preferred violence to law, leaving behind an unfortunate legacy that has polluted international law and aggravated political and diplomatic relations between states. By setting a dangerous precedent (sooner or later, other states could follow this example) and by trampling on the sovereign rights of two allies, the American allowed their emotions to prevail over reason, with negative consequences for all the states involved in the affair.

6

The Attitude of
the Italian Government

Unlike the American Administration, which had already formulated a definite strategy in relation to terrorist attacks, the hijacking of the *Achille Lauro* caught the Italian Government unprepared; the executive had no military or diplomatic 'doctrine' to guide it in handling an international crisis sparked off by a terrorist attack. This was not really a case of bad planning. Rather, despite the recent Palestinian attack in the Via Veneto in Rome on 19 September 1985, Italy did not feel threatened on an *international plane*: the government had been careful to maintain good relations with the various Arab states, including Libya and Syria. Its contribution to the peace-keeping force in Lebanon (Italy had sent a contingent to join the UN forces there in 1983–4) had been appreciated by all the parties involved. Furthermore, its relations with the PLO were also good (only recently, Italy had used strong words to condemn the Israeli attack on the PLO headquarters in Tunis on 1 October 1985).

However, as soon as the news of the hijacking reached Italy, via Göteborg, the Craxi Government immediately devised a strategy and proceeded to apply that strategy consistently, with only a few changes (which became necessary following the Americans' use of force). What were the tenets of this strategy? First, the maintenance of *contact* with all the parties involved, so that no opportunity was missed that could save the lives of the hostages without having to resort to force. Secondly, preparation for a *military intervention*, but only as a last resort. From the outset Italy had decided to apply force only in exceptional circumstances, given that it would have jeopardized the hostages' safety. The government was opposed to this second option for reasons of principle, too: the use of force is not a mainstay of Italian foreign policy. The Italian Government has always believed that international law and the Constitution require it to explore every peaceful way out of an international crisis and, for the most part, has acted accordingly.

Given these two major objectives (the search for a peaceful solution and military action as a last resort), what *specific goals* did the executive pursue during the twists and turns of the crisis?

Italian government action may be divided into various phases, when one objective or another loomed largest. Initially the aim was to *isolate, both politically and diplomatically*, not only the hijackers but their bosses as well. This was achieved the day after the liner was hijacked (namely 8 October), as I remarked in my reconstruction of the facts in chapter 3. Almost from the beginning of the incident, another constant objective was to *prevent the Americans from using force*. By 8 October Washington was already insisting on a military intervention; the Americans were stopped, at least for the time being, only by Craxi's determination. Obviously, Italy could dissuade the Americans from resorting to coercion by using not only forceful legal arguments (after all, the liner was Italian), but diplomatic and political ones as well. However, the Americans' belligerent intentions could be 'contained' only so long as the hijackers were aboard the *Achille Lauro*; once they had disembarked, there was nothing the Italian Government could do to stop the superpower. In point of fact, no sooner was the Egyptian plane in international air space, with the hijackers on board, than the Americans plumped for their 'military option'. The Italians were again able to hold in check the Americans' preference for coercive measures only after the Egyptian Boeing had landed at Sigonella and only so

long as it remained in Italian territory. In this case, the Italian
Government restrained American aggressiveness with quiet
authority, for the excellent reason that the Americans were
breathing fire and brimstone not on home ground but on
territory subject to Italian sovereignty.

Yet another aim was *not to damage Italy's good relations with
the Arab states and the PLO*, the fruits of years of patient
negotiations and contacts. This aim was an integral part of
Italy's Mediterranean policy; an area where Italy feels – quite
rightly, I think – it can play an important political and
diplomatic role (hoping in particular to help find a solution to
the Palestinian question). To this end Italy needs to preserve
good relations with the Arab states and all the other states in
the area, and civil (if not very warm) relations with Israel.

THE STRAIGHT AND NARROW PATH DICTATED BY LAW AND POLICY

All three of the specific objectives I have just outlined in very
brief terms were met with snags and pitfalls that made their
translation into action a slow and difficult process.

First, the government's path had to wend its way down
domestic straits. Italian public opinion was pressing the
government to act promptly and save both the hostages and
the vessel: a contradictory demand, because it was not
possible to bring the hostages safely home by taking instant
action. A policy of keeping all relevant channels open required
patience and slow, considered moves. However, greater
obstacles to the work of the 'crisis committee' in Palazzo Chigi
came from political divisions within the five-party coalition.
One group, led by the imposing figure of the Defence
Minister, Spadolini (Republican), was pro-American and pro-
Israeli. This group wanted to solve the crisis by maintaining
very close contacts with the United States and having little to
do with the PLO, and showed a great readiness to embark on a
military operation. The other group, led by the Prime

Minister, Craxi (Socialist), and by the Foreign Minister, Andreotti (Christian Democrat), did not wish to stand completely in the shadow of 'Big Brother': it wished to give priority to relations with the Arab states – especially Egypt in this case – and to maintain a 'hot line' with the PLO, and Arafat in particular, to persuade him to condemn the hijacking and induce the Palestinian hijackers to surrender.

In addition to these domestic hurdles, the government faced further difficulties of an *international* order. As a member of the North Atlantic Treaty Organization, Italy is politically (if not legally) 'obliged' to coordinate its efforts with those of other countries in the alliance, in this case the United States. On the other hand, its desire to hold sway in the Mediterranean area has often made Italy adopt policies that are not altogether to the liking of America and Israel. These were dangerous waters for the Italian ship of state, between Scylla, in the guise of a break with the Great Alliance, and Charybdis, as the loss of all hope of playing a leading role in the Mediterranean.

Did *law* itself impose certain limitations? Here one must draw a distinction between international rules of conduct and the norms of domestic law. One must also distinguish between the various phases of the incident, because with every change in the political and diplomatic scenery there was a corresponding change in the legal 'channels' to be followed.

At the beginning of the crisis, *Italian law* did not offer clear guidelines and imposed very few limitations. The executive was free to act as it thought best to solve the crisis. Among other things, it could decide not to insist on the extradition of the hijackers, under certain conditions, in the event that they were apprehended by another state. However, the government could not renounce the right of Italian courts to try the hijackers.

In this initial phase, *international law* also offered few points of reference by which to determine government action. The only applicable rule was the general principle that states should endeavour to solve their tensions and conflicts –

whatever their origin – by *peaceful means*. Clearly, this principle leaves plenty of room for manoeuvre. It leaves states free to select the time and the procedures necessary to end a controversy peacefully, as well as the most suitable inter-locutors; it also allows them to choose between alternative peaceful solutions. There is another principle, closely con-nected with the first, that limits the actions of states: the *ban on using, or threatening to use, force, except in certain exceptional circumstances*. The latter includes a serious and immediate threat to the lives of nationals abroad.

Obviously, when the *Achille Lauro* affair began, these two principles provided only very general guidelines, imposing scant limitations on the Italian Government. However, the Italian authorities never once overstepped these limits. Nor was this a particularly arduous task, since the Italian Government has, for years, used them as beacons for its foreign policy, quoting them often – in the UN General Assembly, for example – both to explain the main tenets of Italy's policy in international affairs, and to criticize or condemn other states that had neglected to observe these principles (as, for example, in the case of Israel's attack on the PLO headquarters in Tunis).

As we shall see, the scene changes radically, from a legal point of view, in the subsequent phases of the incident: that is, once the hijackers reached Italian soil after the Americans' military action. From then on, the *applicable international rules* become stringent and precise, as does also the *relevant Italian law*. At this later stage also, Italy's adherence to the dictates of international law becomes rather less scrupulous than before.

TENSION AND CONFLICT WITH THE UNITED STATES

By intercepting the Egyptian Boeing and forcing it to land at Sigonella, the Americans brought about a *radical change* in the *Achille Lauro* affair, both politically, diplomatically and on the legal plane.

From a political and diplomatic point of view they introduced two new factors. First, the tension that already existed between the United States and Italy increased dramatically. This was due to the following circumstances: the Americans' determination to seize the hijackers at Sigonella and fly them to the United States; the violation of Italian territorial sovereignty (as we saw in chapter 3); the American insistence that Abul Abbas be arrested; and their outspoken criticism of the Italian Government when it refused to do so. The second new factor was a worsening of relations with Egypt. Whereas formerly there had been intense collaboration and continuous concerted efforts to find a way out of the crisis, relations now became tense and almost reached breaking-point. Egypt believed that Italy had been wrong in allowing the plane to land at Sigonella; when Italy asked to question the two PLO leaders on board the Boeing, Egypt protested; and the Egyptian Government said it feared that the Americans might 'hijack' the plane again during its flight from Sigonella to Rome. At the same time, the Egyptians decided to keep the *Achille Lauro* 'prisoner' in Port Said as a kind of 'bargaining chip' should the Italians be inclined to give in to American pressure.

From the legal point of view, the change was even more significant. Above all, the behaviour of the various states involved in the affair was no longer inspired by the general principles of international law, but fell within the far more narrow confines of *bilateral treaties*; in particular, the 1983 extradition treaty between the United States and Italy. Thus, the room for manoeuvre left by the general principles of international law was reduced: treaty rules contain far more specific restraints and commands. Further, if until then the governments had acted (or should have acted) according to international rules of conduct, now – at least as far as the Italians were concerned – the rigid rules of Italian criminal law had also to be respected. In consequence, the Italian Government lost its relatively discretionary power and had to refer the matter to the courts, whose duty it is to apply criminal law.

There were now few *alternatives* left open to the Italian Government. Like other parliamentary democracies that respect the principle of 'separation of powers', the Italian Executive cannot interfere with a court's assessment of the facts and its decisions. Thus, the question was no longer one of diplomacy (that is, how to act towards the United States and Egypt) but essentially a domestic question (that is, how to deal with the jurisdiction of Italian criminal courts, which now had a major voice in the matter).

THE ITALIANS DECIDE NOT TO EXTRADITE THE HIJACKERS

Within this general picture, two details should be emphasized: the Italian Government's decision not to allow the extradition of the four hijackers to the United States, and its refusal to carry out the provisional arrest of Abul Abbas. I shall not dwell on how the superpower 'bullied' Italy: the Americans behaved in such a way as to violate Italian sovereignty, giving rise to spirited protests from its Mediterranean cousin and a demand for an official apology which, it seems, was never made, at least not in public.

As to the first point, let me say that the decision not to hand over the four hijackers after their plane had landed at Sigonella was consonant with international law. The 1983 extradition treaty lays down, in Article 3, that when one of the parties requests an extradition for crimes not committed on its territory (as in our case, where the crime was not committed in the United States), then the other party has a discretion whether or not to grant the request. The crime, in this case, was carried out on board an Italian vessel; thus the Italian Government could rightfully refuse to hand over the hijackers on the grounds that it had sufficient evidence to warrant the jurisdiction of the Italian courts.

THE REFUSAL TO ARREST ABUL ABBAS

However, this was not the apple of discord. What rankled was what the Americans regarded as the Italian Government's decision to act for 'reason of state', thereby flagrantly violating international law. The Americans believed they had sufficient proof against Abul Abbas to show that he had masterminded the whole operation or, at least, had directed it ever since the hijackers had decided to sail away from the Syrian coast. That is why the United States had asked the Italian Government to proceed with the 'provisional arrest' of the Palestinian, in accordance with Article 12 of the 1983 treaty.

The Italian Government gave three reasons for rejecting the request. First, the 'evidence' produced by the United States as proof of the Palestinian's guilt was unsubstantial. Secondly, the Egyptian aircraft was 'on a special mission for the Egyptian Government', and therefore enjoyed so-called extra-territorial rights (the Italian authorities could not exercise coercion on board the plane without the captain's consent). Thirdly, Abul Abbas had an Iraqi diplomatic passport and was therefore protected from arrest by diplomatic immunity.

Of these three arguments the most important (but also most questionable) one was the first; the second argument was decisive (at least up to the last stage of the incident); the third was as brittle as glass.

Before we examine each argument in detail, I should like to describe the exact content of the relevant rule in the 1983 treaty and how it applies under Italian law. I hope these introductory remarks may serve to shed light on an extremely confused subject.

How the Italo–American treaty on extradition applies

As I noted earlier, the provision referred to by the Americans in their application for the 'provisional arrest' of Abul Abbas was Article 12. Let us now take a look at this Article.

It provides that 'in case of urgency' each of the contracting parties may apply to the other for the 'provisional arrest' of 'any person charged or convicted of an extraditable offence' (paragraph 1). In paragraph 2, the Article provides that the application for a 'provisional arrest' made by one state (the United States, in this case) to the other (Italy)

shall contain: a description of the person sought including, if available, the person's nationality; the probable location of that person; *a brief statement of the facts of the case including, if possible, the time and location of the offense and the available evidence*; a statement of the existence of a warrant of arrest, with the date it was issued and the name of the issuing court; a description of the type of offenses, a citation to the sections of law violated and the maximum penalty possible upon conviction, or a statement of the existence of a judgment of conviction against that person, with the date of conviction, the name of the sentencing court and the sentence imposed, if any; and a statement that a formal request for extradition of the person sought will follow. (Emphasis added)

The next paragraph provides that 'on receipt of the application, the Requested Party shall take the appropriate steps to secure the arrest [. . .].' The treaty is clearly not very exacting as to the evidence provided; it also requires that the 'requested' state proceed with the 'provisional arrest' so long as the *minimum and essentially formal requisites* are met.

In order to clarify the purport of this provision, it is fitting to stress two points. First, the previous extradition treaty between Italy and the United States, of 1973, was very strict as to the evidence to be produced to support a request for 'provisional arrest': it required that a detailed statement of facts, as well as convincing proof of the alleged crimes, be provided by the requesting state. By contrast, the 1983 treaty is far less demanding. The second point, closely connected with the first, is even more germane to our discussion of the *Achille Lauro* affair. The deletion in the 1983 treaty of the strict requirements as to facts and evidence was effected *at the request* of the *Italian Government*, who believed that those requirements were too stringent or at any rate made it very difficult for the Italian authorities to secure the provisional arrest of alleged criminals living in the United States.

The conclusion can be drawn that in 1983 the loosening of the previous strict requirements was the result of an intentional choice: Italy and the US decided that very little was to be demanded for the purposes of the 'provisional arrest' provided for in Article 12.

However, this is not the end of the matter, for, like any other international rule, this provision does not lead an independent life of its own: it cannot be applied automatically, but must be 'hooked' on to domestic law. In this case, various provisions of Italian law allow the Minister of Justice to evaluate whether all the requirements listed in the second paragraph have been met. As regards the 'provisional arrest' itself, this must be carried out in accordance with Article 663 of the Code of Criminal Procedure, which provides for the arrest of a person whose extradition has either been requested, or is about to be requested. The arrest may be made either by the *polizia giudiziaria*, that is, the enforcement agencies acting under instructions from the judicial authorities (after a warrant has been issued by the public prosecutor of the Court of Appeal or by the public prosecutor of the place where that person is at the time), or by the police (who take their orders from the executive, via the *questore*, or chief of police) 'when the latter receive notice of a warrant, or its equivalent, issued by foreign judicial authorities and the person's departure from the jurisdiction is feared'.

Clearly, the applicability in Italy of Article 12 depends on the relevant Italian domestic rules. These rules provide, in essence, as follows: when the public prosecutor proceeds with the arrest of a person he must first ascertain whether there is 'sufficient evidence' of that person's guilt and whether there is a risk that he or she might indeed abscond. If the arrest is carried out by the police (acting, as I have explained, on orders from the executive), it is then up to the public prosecutor, after a thorough examination of the facts, either to confirm the arrest or to order that the detainee be freed, in particular, the public prosecutor must ascertain whether the necessary conditions for the arrest (ample proof of guilt and of intended escape) do indeed exist.

Now, as I said earlier, the American application, together with its 'documentation', was examined by three judges at the request of the Minister of Justice. They decided that the evidence furnished was *insufficient*.

What was this evidence? (The American documentation is no longer secret because it was produced as evidence before the Genoa Court of Assizes: according to one of the fundamental principles of Italian criminal procedure, once a trial has been held the transcripts and evidence are no longer confidential.) First, there was a request from the FBI sent, via Interpol, to the Italian intelligence service and to the Ministry of the Interior. The request merely stated that 'the United States Department of Justice had received information it considered useful, because it proved that Abul Abbas had taken part in the hijacking of the *Achille Lauro*', adding that 'the United States Government will try to make this information available to the Italian Government.' Slightly longer, though no more 'substantial', was the *formal application* which the US Embassy sent to the Italian Minister of Justice. In Note no. 1056, of 12 October 1985, Ambassador Rabb merely reported that Judge Charles R. Richey, of the District Court of the District of Columbia, had issued a warrant for the arrest of Abul Abbas on the basis of three separate charges (hostage-taking, piracy under the law of nations, conspiracy); he then indicated the penalty for each offence under US law. As to the proof of his guilt, the Note merely stated that 'the facts show that Abul Abbas conspired with the four hijackers to hijack the Italian ship [. . .]'.

However sparse the 'documentation' produced by the Americans, the Italian Minister of Justice decided not to rest content with the decision of the three judges. Both Craxi, in his speech on 17 October, and the Genoa Court of Assizes, state that the American application was immediately sent by the Minister of Justice to the two public prosecutors that had jurisdiction in the hijacking affair: Genoa and Syracuse. By so doing the government enabled the two public prosecutors to examine whether Article 663 applied to the case. Had they decided to issue a warrant for Abul Abbas' arrest, they could have ordered the police to arrest him. And yet, after consideration of all the evidence, both offices reported back to Rome (as noted in chapter 3) that they felt they could not authorize the arrest. The office in Genoa stated as follows: 'We submit that at present there are not sufficient grounds to allow this office to issue a warrant against Abul Abbas, as having taken part in the hijacking of the liner *Achille Lauro* and the taking of hostages.'

Undoubtedly, the two public prosecutors did not merely carry out a perfunctory examination of the application for the 'provisional arrest', but inquired into Abul Abbas' involvement in the whole incident. In other words, they took the Americans' 'documentation' as their starting point to discover whether the necessary proof of crime existed that would justify a measure restricting the Palestinian's freedom.

The barriers set up by international customary law

So far I have shown how the Italian Government was prevented from accepting the American application because Italian judges – whose job it is to decide whether or not the preconditions for the application of Article 12 are met in each specific case – had decided that in the case of Abul Abbas those preconditions were not met.

Did the Italian authorities use Italian criminal law as an excuse not to perform an international duty? Were this true they would have violated the 1983 treaty: one incontrovertible principle of international law proclaims that a state cannot invoke its own law as an excuse for the breach of an international duty. If one of its laws prevents it from carrying out that international duty, then the state must either repeal or modify its own legislation; if it does not do so it commits an unlawful act under international law.

Undoubtedly, a *discrepancy* does exist between Article 12 of the 1983 treaty (which only insists on minimum requirements) and Italian criminal law (which is extremely rigorous if it is interpreted and applied correctly). Nevertheless, in the case at hand, Italy committed no wrong – at least, not up until the final stage, as I shall explain later. Article 12 must be *interpreted in the light of other international rules*, especially those general norms on the limits of a territorial state's power with regard to areas and possessions that enjoy 'extraterritorial' rights.

Perhaps the reason why this norm must be coordinated with other international rules will be clearer if I invert the roles: suppose Italy requests the US Government to apply Article 12 and carry out the 'provisional arrest' of a Colombian who has committed serious crimes against Italian nationals and has then taken refuge in the Columbian Embassy in Washington. Although the American courts can issue a warrant, the US police may not arrest the Colombian. The Columbian Embassy premises enjoy diplomatic immunity (under the theory of 'extraterritoriality') and, unless the embassy agrees to hand over the Colombian, or allows the US police to come in and arrest him, the American authorities have their hands tied. As a consequence, the United States cannot apply the bilateral treaty with Italy. In this regard it does not commit an international delinquency because compliance with the provisions of Article 12 would entail disregarding an international duty owed to Columbia, which that state alone can agree to waive. Putting this a different way, international law does not allow states to apply their bilateral agreements in such a way as to prejudice the rights of third states.

In our case, the international rules that had to be applied in conjunction with Article 12 were those concerning the limits to the judicial and coercive powers of one state over another state's *ships* and *aircraft* on a *military* or *official mission*. This was the basis for the second reason Craxi gave for the government's impotence in applying Article 12 – that the Egyptian aircraft enjoyed 'extraterritoriality'. The Italian Government did not 'invent' this argument: it had been explicitly advanced by the Egyptian Government. This emerges quite clearly from the report of Craxi's diplomatic adviser, Mr Badini, of his 'meeting' with Abul Abbas. He emphasizes how, in explaining the position of his government, the Egyptian Ambassador had insisted that the Egyptian aircraft was 'on a special state mission' and therefore enjoyed diplomatic immunity. The ambassador added that this immunity meant that Abul Abbas could not even be questioned by the Italian judicial authorities; and he went so far as to point out that there were ten armed guards on board the aircraft, ready to ensure that this 'immunity' was respected.

This argument is entirely convincing (subject to what I shall say in the next section), because it is true that when an aircraft is on an official mission the authorities of the state where the plane has landed cannot perform any judicial or coercive act without the permission of the captain, or of the diplomatic officials of the state to which the plane belongs.

Before asking whether the Italian Executive still had some room for manoeuvre, let us just take a look at Craxi's third argument, which he advanced to *back up* the second. This was that Abul Abbas was inviolable because he held an Iraqi quasi-diplomatic passport: even if it had been possible to board the plane, which it was not, the Palestinian could not have been arrested, or even asked to give evidence, without violating the immunity that all diplomatic envoys enjoy. As I indicated earlier, this argument is very flimsy indeed. No one doubts that diplomats are 'sacred': as Montesquieu said, they 'are the word of the prince who sent them, and this word must be free'. But Palestinian officials with diplomatic passports cannot be equated with 'diplomatic agents' in the normal sense of that term. Some Arab states do give Palestinian leaders passports, known as *passeports de complaisance*. This does not mean that these Palestinians act as the diplomatic agents of that state, since the latter gave them the passport only to make it easier for them to get about. A diplomatic passport gives its holder the right to enjoy diplomatic privileges only after a complex procedure has been followed: the presentation of credentials by the envoy to the receiving state and his acceptance by that state as a *persona grata*. Abul Abbas had never been accredited by Iraq to any state, or even to any international organization. In other words, he could not enjoy diplomatic immunity as a 'diplomat in transit' (albeit enforced transit). The duty to grant diplomatic privileges and immunity to a 'diplomat in transit' applies only to a person crossing the territory of a third state 'while proceeding to take up or return to his post, or when returning to his own country' (Article 40, paragraph 1, of the 1961 Vienna Convention on Diplomatic Relations). Abul Abbas was not proceeding to another state to take up a diplomatic post there; nor, having taken up such a post, was he returning to his country of origin.

The United States accuses Italy of violating the extradition treaty

To return to the 1983 treaty, we have seen how the Italian authorities took the view that the American application for Abul Abbas' 'provisional arrest' did not comply with all the preconditions in Article 12 of that treaty and that, in addition, they were prevented by customary international law from carrying out that arrest.

The United States took a contrary view. On 13 October 1985 the White House issued a harshly-worded statement, commenting on the decision of the Italian Government in the following terms: '[the Italian] judicial authorities did not consider [the United States'] evidence legally strong enough to support the provisional arrest of Abbas while awaiting a formal US request for his extradition . . . the US government is astonished at this breach of any reasonable standard of due process and is deeply disappointed.' Equally critical was a statement made by Judge Sofaer in an interview held that day. He asserted that Italy *had violated its international obligations* in letting Abul Abbas go, saying:

The [1983] treaty conferred upon them [the Italians] a clear duty to hold Abbas until we had been given a fair opportunity to present the evidence we had against him. We went in the middle of the night, we accumulated as much evidence as we could in 24 hours. We got a complaint, we got a warrant. We sent the papers to Italy with a summary of our evidence. We told them that more was coming, more is accumulating every hour, but they did not wait. They rushed, made a decision, and let him go.

It is my contention that the United States was right in accusing Italy of violating the 1983 treaty. The Italian breach resulted from a wrong interpretation of Article 12 by the Italian judges, as well as the failure of the Italian enforcement agencies to arrest Abul Abbas as soon as he left the Egyptian aircraft, that is to say, as soon as he ceased to benefit from the 'extraterritorial immunity' enjoyed by the aircraft. Let me consider these two points separately.

Admittedly, the Italian criminal law is very strict as far as the provisional arrest of a person suspected of having committed a crime is concerned. I have mentioned before the provisions of the Italian code of criminal procedure which demand that a judge pass upon the evidence available and the risk of escape, and permit the arrest of a suspect only if solid evidence against him exists and only on condition that he is likely to abscond. True, the Italian judges and other competent state agencies called upon to apply Article 12 of the 1983 treaty must take account of the relevant Italian provisions governing criminal procedure. However, in view of the discrepancy between Article 12 and the much more stringent Italian rules, the Italian authorities should have taken account of the fact that Article 12 should prevail on two counts: first, it is embodied in an international treaty constituting *lex specialis* with respect to Italian criminal procedure; secondly, it is subsequent to those Italian norms, that is, it is *lex posterior*. In these circumstances the most appropriate course for the Italian authorities would have been simply to construe the relevant rules of the Italian code of criminal procedure in such a way as to render them consistent with Article 12. To put this another way, the loose requirements laid down in Article 12, rather than the stringent domestic ones, should have been taken by the Italian judges as the yardstick by which to gauge whether or not the request of the American authorities concerning Abul Abbas was acceptable. As a consequence the Italian judges should have complied with that request, although, as long as Abul Abbas was in the Egyptian plane, they were in fact unable to take the coercive measures needed, on account of the international rule on the 'extraterritorial immunity' of the aircraft.

Let us now turn to the measures taken by the Italian Government. As long as Abul Abbas was in the Egyptian plane they could not order the Italian enforcement agencies to enter the plane. Were other avenues open to Italy? The Italian Government faced a difficult problem, posed by the strict (and, as I have indicated, in my view misconceived) interpretation placed by the Italian judges on the 1983 treaty. How could it comply with the American request without interfering with, and indeed disregarding, the decisions of the Italian judiciary?

I should mention here that on the morning of 12 October, when Ambassador Rabb learnt of the doubts and reservations of the Italian judicial authorities about the documentation sent from Washington, he clutched at one last straw. He promised that new and more convincing documents would very soon arrive from Washington. And so they did, the very next day – that is, the day after Abul Abbas left Rome for Yugoslavia. Unfortunately, from the point of view of criminal procedure, this documentation was equally unsubstantial. All it did was to mention a number of facts, based on so-called 'reliable information', without backing these up with any concrete proof. The second batch of evidence was so flimsy that the Genoa Court of Assizes remarked that the American 'documentation' was of no relevance in determining Abul Abbas' crimes. (As I pointed out in chapter 3, the inquiring magistrate in Genoa had already stated as much.) However, this assessment was made *after the event*.

One wonders whether the government should not have

been prompted, by the Americans' application for a 'provisional arrest' and the promise of new and more convincing documents, to *prevent for a few days the Egyptian aircraft from leaving Fiumicino airport*, or at least to *stop Abul Abbas from leaving Rome*. If the Italian authorities were determined to allow their *judges* to weigh the new documentation, they could still have begun negotiations to these ends with the Egyptians because, as I have indicated, the Boeing could not leave the airport, nor Abul Abbas the plane, without the Italians' consent. True, the Egyptian Government was keeping the *Achille Lauro* in Port Said. But the crew and passengers had little to fear from a state that, far from being hostile to Italy, was involved in negotiations with it. However intricate and delicate, negotiations between Cairo and Rome might have produced a solution that gave the Italian judges time to examine the new American documentation. If the proof had turned out to be compelling, the Italian authorities might have been able to *convince* their counterparts in Egypt to *waive the immunity* enjoyed by those in the plane, or to hand over Abul Abbas. Admittedly, had the Americans produced *decisive* evidence, this would not have had the automatic and obligatory effect of forcing the Italians to proceed with the arrest: the rule on 'extraterritoriality' remained an obstacle. Nevertheless, such evidence might have had an indirect effect: the Italians could have used it to put pressure on the Egyptians and induce them to waive the immunity.

Thus, the Italian Government did have a 'safe' option from the legal point of view: it could have kept Abul Abbas in Rome, without violating the rule on 'extraterritoriality' as far as the Egyptian aircraft was concerned, or disregarding the interpretation of the rules of Italian criminal procedure advanced by the Italian judges.

This would certainly have been more consistent with the *spirit* of the treaty with the United States, and the *principles of friendly cooperation* that should exist between states, especially when they are allies. Instead, the Italian executive used its restricted (domestic) discretionary power to ignore the

American requests, while lending an ear to the Egyptians.

Further, while the Italian Government's breach of the 1983 treaty may have been excusable at the beginning (on account of the customary rule on extraterritoriality), it was no longer excusable once Abul Abbas left the Egyptian aircraft and was allowed to board the Yugoslav plane. The Italian Executive should have ordered the police to proceed with the provisional arrest of Abul Abbas, as requested by the United States, the moment the immunity attaching to the aircraft no longer sheltered him. True, the Palestinian left the Boeing only after the Italian authorities had formally promised the Egyptian Government that the Italian police would not violate its immunity. This formal promise was, in effect, a *bilateral agreement* entered into by Italy with Egypt. In a sense, this agreement was implicitly confirmed and reiterated by the Italian Government when it notified the Egyptian and American ambassadors – on Saturday 12 October at 3 p.m. – that 'there was no reason to detain the airliner and its passengers any longer'; only later, at about 7 p.m., did Abul Abbas board the Yugoslav plane. The fact remains, however, that this agreement was a breach of the 1983 treaty with the United States.

The conclusion is therefore warranted that the Italian Government, partly also because of the misconceived interpretation on the part of the Italian judges, first behaved in a manner contrary to the spirit of the 1983 treaty and the basic principle of friendly cooperation between allies, and then committed an outright violation of Article 12 of the treaty. What was the reason for this behaviour?

The political and diplomatic motives that inspired the Craxi government

I think there were at least four non-legal reasons for the attitude of the Italian authorities. Two of these were 'selfish' and inspired by short-term national interests. The other two reflected political and diplomatic needs that transcend purely national interests.

To some extent, I have already referred to the first two. The authorities did not want the arrest of Abul Abbas to set off a chain of terrorist violence against Italian nationals, interests and possessions. Had he been arrested and tried, the PLF would certainly have attempted to avenge their leader by striking blindly at innocent Italians. (These fears were well grounded: on 12 October the Palestinian press agency in Tunis, Wafa, announced that Arafat had sent Craxi a warning not to hand over Abbas to the Americans, because this 'could provoke uncontrollable reactions, such as those that had happened during the *Achille Lauro* incident, after the Americans' act of piracy against the Egyptian aircraft.') The second reason was that the Egyptians were not prepared to let the Italian liner leave Port Said for Italy and finally put a stop to the whole drama. The third reason was of a political and diplomatic nature. Egypt was in the midst of a major political crisis. The Americans had so humiliated the Egyptians by intercepting the Boeing 737 that the extremist factions, which were already highly critical of the government's pro-American policy, had become inflamed. The precarious Mubarak Government was now close to breaking point. This is why the Egyptians sent their very able and energetic ambassador to Rome post-haste to protest that their plane had been kept on at Sigonella after the four hijackers had been arrested, and had later been forced to go on to Rome. With every passing hour, the fact that the two Palestinian leaders and the aircraft had not yet been released increased fears of repercussions in Cairo. The Americans' 'smack in the face' was being aggravated by a further 'offence' to Egyptian sovereignty by Italy. The grave danger to the stability of the Egyptian Government was a determining factor in the Italians' decision to act quickly and no longer to heed the American requests for 'time'.

There may have been one last reason for the Italians' actions, at least in the opinion of the *New York Times*. In the heat of the moment, that newspaper wrote in a political commentary that Italy (like Egypt and Yugoslavia) believed the arrest of an important Palestinian leader might have had extremely negative effects on the PLO, and equally pernicious repercussions on efforts to achieve peace in the Middle East. The PLO would probably have been wrecked by infighting. This would have shattered its prestige and authority and strengthened all those states that wished to exclude any Palestinian group from negotiations for a solution of the Middle East question.

I do not know if this interpretation is correct. However, those fears, if they existed, have proved to be without foundation, given recent developments inside the PLO and improved relations between the PLO and Jordan. Undoubtedly, an opportunity to forestall terrorist attacks in Italy and to free the *Achille Lauro* from its harrowing ordeal, not to mention the need to help the Mubarak Government stay afloat, all outweighed, as far as the Italian Government was concerned, the need to discover the extent of Abbas' guilt in masterminding or at least controlling the hijacking. And, of course, these reasons, which certainly underlay Italy's attitude to the 1983 treaty (first a rather formalistic and rigid application of Article 12, then its outright breach), were also a determining factor in inducing Italy to abide by an important general principle of international law: the 'extraterritoriality' of certain property of foreign states (in this case an Egyptian aircraft on an official mission).

In the end, one cannot escape the conclusion that Italy observed international law during the affair when observance suited it politically. Certainly, it was scrupulous in its observance of the international rules regarding resort to force, managing to avoid force entirely. However, when, during the final stages of the affair, the legal basis for its non-observance of treaty obligations owed to the United States evaporated, Italy carried on regardless, apparently preferring political expediency to the dictates of justice and legal propriety.

7

The Italian Judges' Verdict

INTRODUCTION

Italian justice and the Italian police (*polizia giudiziaria*) were quick to act. The four hijackers arrested at Sigonella underwent a thorough interrogation, while the police also conducted investigations throughout Italy and arrested other Palestinians, charged with having taking part, more or less directly, in the hijacking operation. At the same time, warrants were issued for the arrest of terrorists still at large (including Abul Abbas) for having instigated or planned the hijacking. Unfortunately, the latter had all escaped abroad and it was no longer possible to bring them before the court.

At the end of the investigations, conducted with speed and efficiency, three of the hijackers (their leader, Al Molqi Magied, and two Palestinians whose work was mainly to guard the hostages held in the 'tapestry saloon' of the *Achille Lauro*, Fataier Abdelatif Ibrahim and Al Assadi Ahmad Marouf) appeared before the Genoa Court of Assizes. The fourth, Al Asker Bassam (who could speak English and had spent most of the time with Captain De Rosa, acting as an interpreter) proved to have been a *minor* during the hijacking. His case was referred to the Juvenile Court in Genoa. Ten other terrorists (including Abul Abbas, Ziad El Omar and Ozzudin Badraktan, who had sponsored and masterminded the operation) had to be tried and convicted *in absentia* because they had absconded.

After a lengthy hearing, the Court gave its verdict on 10

July 1986: the three instigators I have just mentioned were given life sentences. The hijacker who murdered Klinghoffer (Al Molqi) was sentenced to thirty years' imprisonment. Shorter sentences were meted out to the other accused. The sentences were later lengthened by the Appellate Court of Assizes. Al Asker Bassam was sentenced by the Juvenile Court to sixteen years and three months imprisonment; this sentence was later increased by the Court of Appeal, Juvenile Section.

I should warn readers that from now on I shall refer mainly to the verdict of the Court of Assizes, because it undoubtedly contains the most wide-ranging and detailed analysis of the 'facts', as well as advancing excellent legal arguments. A few months after the first verdict, the judges of the Juvenile Court gave a decision to a large extent based on, or even copied from, the earlier one. As for the two Courts of Appeal, I shall examine their judgments only in so far as they *disagree* with the approach of the Court of Assizes, the main point of disagreement being the question of whether the hijackers had formed a *banda armata* and were therefore to be considered criminals quite independently of the crimes of hijacking, hostage-taking and murder, of which they stood accused.

Furthermore, I must warn the reader that I shall always refer to the 'judges', even though in Italy a Court of Assizes is made up of a jury and two judges.

THE APPROACH OF THE COURT OF ASSIZES

What problems did the Genoese judges have to face? Naturally, the Italian government's action (its contacts with other interested states and with the PLO, as well as the conclusion of the safe-conduct agreement) did not fall within the scope of their inquiry. Nor were they required legally to assess the Americans' actions in intercepting the Egyptian Boeing, or their conduct at Sigonella and in the air space between Sicily and Ciampino airport. The judges had to try the members of a terrorist commando, together with their instigators and accomplices, for the hijacking, for Klinghoffer's murder and for other crimes committed on board the liner. Thus, the scope of their inquiry was fairly restricted. Moreover, they were called upon to apply *Italian criminal law*. Since the crimes had been committed on board an Italian vessel, even though the victims were of different nationalities, the norms of Italian penal law were fully applicable. The Genoese judges decided that there was no need to draw on the rules of *international law* to issue a verdict on the conduct of the Palestinians.

This may seem a surprising decision. In point of fact, the Court had to decide on one crucial question, the answer to which was to be found mainly in international law: were the hijackers mere *terrorists* (and as such liable to the penalties foreseen in the Italian criminal code for ordinary crimes), or were they *lawful combatants* in a war of national liberation (and as such exempt, under certain strict conditions, from these penalties because their action was justified under international law)? Clearly, the question was of a 'transnational' nature: the most relevant rules and principles by which to solve it were, surely, those that regulate relations between states and between these and other bodies (individuals, groups, peoples, national liberation movements) that have a part – often only a walk-on part – to play on the international stage. Indeed, the judges should really have determined whether nowadays international law considers actions such as the hijacking of the *Achille Lauro* legitimated as part of the struggle of the Palestinian people for self-determination. Had they decided this was so, then Italian criminal law would no longer have applied; had they decided it was not so, the hijacking would have fallen entirely under their jurisdiction.

I should at once explain that the fact that the criminal law of a state refers back to the rules of the international community is by no means a new phenomenon. Similarly, during hostilities between states, acts that, under the criminal law of one of the belligerents, should be tried as *ordinary crimes* (the destruction of the possessions and military installations of another state; the capture, detention and killing of the citizens of another state, etc.) are considered *legitimate* because they are justified by the *international laws of war*.

Had the judges decided to examine the question from the vantage-point of international law they would have had to take into account recent developments in the international rules governing hostilities. They would have discovered that international law tends more and more to equate *wars of national liberation* with *wars between states*: thus, those who fight for the freedom of their homeland must be treated, on certain conditions, as the members of a regular army at war with another state. The Genoese judges would have faced a twofold question. First, did the hijacking form part of a war of liberation recognized as 'legitimate' and *therefore equated with a war between states?* Secondly, if this first condition was fulfilled, did the hijackers satisfy the *other conditions* that are necessary under international law for a 'hostile action' to be considered legitimate, hence not an ordinary crime?

As I have said, the Court in Genoa felt these queries should be posed exclusively in the ambit of Italian criminal law. It is easy to disagree with this interpretation. But, as we shall see, what counts is that the Court's findings were, by and large, satisfactory and not very different from those it might have made after extending its examination of the law into the international field.

On the whole, one cannot but praise the Court. It handed down a wise and balanced judgment. By an intelligent application of certain concepts of Italian criminal law, the judges condemned the hijackers and their leaders without, however, ignoring the social and political environment from which this act of terrorism sprang: the war the Palestinians have been waging for decades to win back their homeland and create a state of their own. Furthermore, the Court must be commended for having conducted a penetrating inquiry into the facts and their background: what led up to the idea of the hijacking, and the political and ideological motives of the Palestinian groups that took part in it. In sum, the Genoese judges wanted to probe those dramatic events and discover why the *Achille Lauro* was hijacked in the first place. From this point of view the judgment made a valuable contribution to the accurate identification of the facts threw new light on certain aspects of the conflict in the Middle East.

THE COURT'S FINDINGS AS TO THE FACTS

I have just remarked that one of the merits of the judges' reasoning is that they managed to disentangle the cat's cradle that was the *Achille Lauro* affair. They were fully aware of how important it was to 'decipher' the facts and started their judgement with the words: 'only by reconstructing the various phases of the operation – its conception, planning, organization and completion – will it be possible to pinpoint and distinguish the exact responsibility of each of the accused involved in it, even if only marginally so.'

In particular, the Genoa Court made a decisive contribution on two important points: the relations between Abul Abbas' group and the PLO, as well as the real objective of the hijacking (the link between the alleged terrorist action in the Israeli port of Ashdod and the hijacking of the Italian liner). Let me give a brief outline of how the judges helped to clarify these two points.

Relations between the PLF and the PLO

First, let us see exactly what the Court discovered about relations between the instigators of the hijacking and the PLO. On the basis of the consistent evidence given by the accused, as well as various documents produced during the trial, the judges concluded that the Palestine Liberation Front (PLF) 'directed by Abul Abbas' was *alone* responsible for planning and carrying out the terrorist operation; the PLO and Arafat had no connection whatever with the conception, planning and execution of the operation: Arafat, in particular, became involved only after the ship had been hijacked and only as a mediator, trying to find a peaceful solution.

The Court deduced that Abul Abbas had planned the operation from the following circumstances. First, it emerged from the evidence of the defendants that Al Molqi , who led the commando, had gone to Tunis to receive his instructions from Abul Abbas on how to conduct the operation; these instructions were then reiterated in a letter 'in Abul Abbas' own handwriting' containing 'plans for the action and the orders to be obeyed'; the letter was sent to Genoa and opened by the hijackers on board the *Achille Lauro*. Al Molqi himself told the inquiring magistrate that the operation aboard the *Achille Lauro* had been 'planned secretly by Abul Abbas, unbeknown to Arafat. The action was carried out without Arafat's being informed because of political rivalry about which I know nothing.' Secondly, the camps where the hijackers had been trained were organized by the PLF and run by men from that group. Thirdly, 'all the accused involved in the organizational phase' belonged exclusively to the PLF.

The Court also considered another point (raised by one of the counsel for the victims): how could the whole crime have been conceived and carried out without Arafat's knowing anything about it? If the PLF is just one of the groups belonging to the PLO, how can the head of that organization have been kept in the dark? The Court was quite clear on this point. What emerged from the trial was that the PLF (which the Court identified with Abul Abbas) enjoys considerable political, strategic and operational autonomy from the PLO; further, its objectives are in many respects at odds with those of Arafat's Organization. The Court deduced this from various facts. For example, the PLF was itself in direct contact with the Tunisian Government: it did not have to go through the parent organization. In September 1985 the PLF held its seventh conference in Tunis, during which Abul Abbas was re-elected secretary general for the group. As the Court remarked, 'the very fact of holding a conference seems to be significant proof of that organization's autonomy from the

PLO.' But the most important element was the open political disagreement between the PLF and the PLO. One of the defendants, Al Asker Bassam, told the Court: 'We chose to be led by Abul Abbas, because we felt Arafat's policy was too soft, since he had agreed to negotiate with our enemies.' Another of the accused, Al Assadi, told the Court that 'the difference between the PLO and the PLF is as great as between the sky and the earth.' Essentially, Abul Abbas was against Arafat because he was prepared to talk to the various leaders in the Middle East, and above all because Arafat was ready to cooperate with Jordan: the *Achille Lauro* operation was intended to sabotage Arafat's strategy, to drive a wedge between Egypt and the United States, and to give a radical twist to the struggle for the liberation of Palestine.

The Palestinian commando's real objective

In my opinion, in reconstructing the facts, the Court's greatest contribution was to investigate whether the commando had originally planned to carry out a terrorist attack in the Israeli port of Ashdod, as – at least from 9 October – they claimed, or whether the hijacking had always been the sole objective of the operation. After a detailed analysis of the facts, the Court came firmly to the view that the idea of a terrorist action in Ashdod was a 'smokescreen'; *from the very beginning, the only operation planned by Abul Abbas was the hijacking of the Italian liner.* The Court gave five reasons for this conclusion.

First, the versions of the proposed terrorist attack in Ashdod given by the various accused contradicted one another. A careful comparison of all the versions persuaded the Court that not only were there discrepancies in the statements of the various accused, but the same man one day would contradict his own version of the facts at the next interrogation. This could only mean that there was no precise plan for an attack at Ashdod, for the simple reason that the action was only a 'cover'.

The second reason was even more decisive: the contradictory versions as to why it had been decided to change plans and hijack the liner instead. On this point, the Court stated the following:

In some versions, those of Al Molqi and Fataier, and once that of Al Asker too, they claimed to have changed plan because they had been discovered, weapons in hand, by one of the stewards. According to this version, the steward was tied and gagged and the idea of the hijacking was born and promptly carried out. These versions turned out not to be true; this episode on board the ship never took place. Al Assadi, and then Al Asker too, absolutely denied that they had ever been discovered by a steward or that they had reacted in the manner described, and gagged the steward. On this point, Al Molqi and Fataier gave confused and contradictory versions (during the trial, Al Molqi denied being present at the alleged discovery, Fataier said the man had not been gagged). The declarations of Al Assadi and Al Asker as to the falsity of the alleged episode are repeatedly corroborated by the witnesses' evidence. The captain and the other officers of the ship say they never heard a word about it; the stewards who looked after the four hijackers' cabin denied there was any truth in it, the other members of the crew, in their evidence before the inquiring magistrate and at the trial, all agreed they had no direct or indirect knowledge of it.

The third point was that, before the conversation via radio (on 9 October) between the head of the commando, Al Molqi, and Abul Abbas (then in Port Said), none of the hijackers had told the captain, who had been in continual contact with two of the Palestinians (Al Molqi and Al Asker), that their real objective had been to disembark at Ashdod. The only logical conclusion is that this 'smokescreen' was put up on orders from Abul Abbas, after the hijacking had failed because the Syrians had refused to cooperate.

The fourth reason was that the whole operation was well timed. When the four hijackers took over the ship, roughly six hundred passengers had left (disembarking at Alexandria for a trip to the pyramids); of those that remained all, or almost all, were in the dining room and, therefore, easy to control. As the Court pointed out, it is hard to believe that the hijacking was a makeshift solution thought up on the spur of the moment. Everything, the timing, the speed and synchronization of the hijackers' movements, their perfect knowledge of the crucial areas of the ship, cannot be reconciled with an 'unforeseen' and 'impromptu' operation.

However convincing these four arguments, what settles the matter once and for all is that such action in the port of Ashdod would have been virtually impossible. Apparently, both Abul Abbas and Al Molqi were fully aware of this. Here is what the Court stated on this point:

To land at Ashdod, according to the several plans ventilated by Al Molqi and the others, would not have been possible. The arms, implements and munitions possessed by the squad (four Kalashnikov machine guns, each with three magazines; eight pineapple hand grenades and nine detonators) were totally inadequate for such an operation, which required intense and continuous fire (Al Asker, surprised at how inadequate these arms were, remarked 'every fedajn is normally given five magazines per machine gun, and we were given only three'). In any case the checks carried out by the Israeli agents before passengers are allowed to land at the port are so thorough and efficient that not only would the four never have got off the ship, but they would never have got as far as the gangplank. On this point, the evidence given during the inquiries by the witnesses . . . is extremely significant. This evidence proves that the checks are carried out in two phases. The first phase concerns those people who have booked a landing. The examination of passports and their owners is so rigorous that the four, with their false passports, physical appearance and ignorance of foreign languages (only Al Asker knew some English), would never have got through the control. For example, according to the witnesses, the [Israeli] officials could certainly not have missed the fact that Fataier, who looks typically Middle Eastern and speaks only Arabic, could not pass for a Norwegian called Stale Wan, as his passport declared. The second phase concerns the same people as they are about to leave the ship. The control is so stringent that any surprise or violent action is virtually impossible for anyone who has gone through the control and, even more so, for anyone trying to get off without having had his passport checked. As to how thorough these checks were, Vignali [one of the witnesses] gave very detailed evidence during the trial: 'Outside the harbour of Ashdod an Israeli patrol-boat comes alongside with some men in plain-clothes from the security services, extremely heavily armed . . . they take over all the key points of the ship . . . before the passengers are allowed to disembark they are shepherded into a hall . . . the only way onto the gangplank is through this hall where there are men checking people . . . if you wanted to slip through and get off, they'd block you on board in the hall . . . there are always at least ten [officials] . . . they take over the hall and the gangplank . . . there are paratroopers scattered around the quay . . . previously the ship is checked by frogmen.' Now, the fact that it was absolutely impossible for the members of the squad, not only to get off at the port, but even to get anywhere near the gangway leading off the ship, in other words, the fact that it was impossible to carry out the projected operation, was certainly well known to the organizers of the hijacking. Certainly, the operation would have been of the 'suicide' type, but it is also true that such operations require that, before dying, as many of the enemy as possible are killed and maximum damage is wrought. In our case, as we have seen, neither of these requirements could have been fulfilled, not only because the arms and munitions were totally inadequate, but, above all, because of the extremely stringent security measures adopted by the Israelis.

Thus, the Court gave five very solid reasons for refuting the theory put forward by Abul Abbas and the hijackers. But, if the Ashdod operation was no more than a 'smokescreen' created to conceal the real objective (the hijacking of the *Achille Lauro*), why did Abul Abbas invent such a story? The Court also examined this question. It believed there were two main reasons for the deception. The first was that the hijacking was to take place unbeknown to Arafat – because its aim was to increase Abbas' prestige and give him a political advantage within the PLO. Arafat would certainly have stopped it, for the very good reason that the ship belonged to a country that was 'friendly' to the PLO. The second – 'additional' – reason was that as few people as possible should know about the real objective of the operation for it to succeed; this might explain why the other members of the commando were kept in the dark. In my view the Court's analysis is unsatisfactory in this regard: there must have been other, more compelling reasons why Abul Abbas 'invented' an action in the port of Ashdod, which he knew to be impossible.

If, as the Court pointed out, it was vital to keep the hijacking secret to prevent Arafat from blocking it, why, once the hijacking had been carried out, did Abul Abbas feel he had to contrive the Ashdod cover? Admittedly, the letter of secret instructions on the Ashdod operation, which Abbas sent to Genoa with one of his men, may well have been intended to 'mislead' Arafat, had it fallen into the hands of the PLO. But why insist obsessively on the abortive action against the Israelis *after* the Italian ship had been hijacked and Abbas' real objective achieved?

I think there was another reason for the 'double objective'. PLO strategy, approved by Arafat and by many authoritative members of the Organization, is based on the idea that the Palestinians' war of national liberation legitimizes military action *against the Israelis, on Israeli territory or in Arab territory occupied by Israel.* Arafat has always declared that terrorist actions, that is, actions against innocent persons, especially if they involve the unarmed nationals of any state other than Israel, are not legitimate. This policy, which the PLO proclaimed as early as 1974, has been reiterated often in recent times, both before and after the hijacking of the Italian ship. Plainly, this policy was determined by an important factor: the increasingly unambiguous condemnation of terrorist action by the international community; states now tend to form a united front against terrorism. As I pointed out in chapter 1, this front crystallized in 1985, after a resolution was passed unanimously both by the General Assembly and by the Security Council of the United Nations.

If the behaviour of the Palestinian commando is viewed in this light, it is quite clear that Abul Abbas' group – who probably never really agreed with the PLO policy just referred to – had to justify an act of terrorism, by insisting that it was merely a *fall back* solution, intended to replace a military operation against Israel which would have fulfilled all the requirements of official PLO strategy. In other words, Abul Abbas was launching an operation that would have undermined the PLO's prestige and Arafat's contacts with Jordan and Egypt; at the same time, he felt he must *justify* it – in the eyes of PLO leaders, a group to which he belonged, for better or worse – by making a series of statements that rendered the terrorist action, to some extent, compatible with the official 'political philosophy' of the Organization. By so doing, the PLF leader killed two birds with one stone: he undermined Arafat's power and credibility, as well as undertaking an action that would sabotage Arafat's attempts at peaceful negotiations; moreover, this fiction provided an easy escape route from the indignity of being condemned by the majority group within the PLO for having deviated drastically from official policy.

This also serves to explain why Abul Abbas obeyed Arafat's orders to go to Cairo to convince the four hijackers to give themselves up. (As the judges noted, in an interview with the Arab weekly *Al Zatan Al Arabi*, published in Paris [No. 453, 18–24 October 1985], Abul Abbas said: 'My trip to and from Egypt was forced.') It is also the reason why Arafat was unable to apply any 'sanctions' to the PLF leader. Finally, it explains why, in a recent interview in Algiers (with the Greek daily, *Ta Nea*, on 17 February 1987), Abul Abbas aired his theory once again: 'We wanted to carry out a military operation against Israel and we failed.' The hijacking of the Italian liner was also – according to Abul Abbas – a failure, but 'if necessary we shall not hesitate to organize another operation like it.'

WERE THE HIJACKERS TERRORISTS OR 'FREEDOM FIGHTERS'?

Let us now see how the judges dealt with the legal issues raised by the hijacking of the *Achille Lauro* and Klinghoffer's murder. As I noted earlier, the Court chose to examine the charges on the basis of *Italian criminal law*. How, then, did the Court solve the complex legal issues of the case within these 'domestic' confines?

Of the many problems the judges had to face, three stood out. First, was the hijacking of the Italian liner an act of terrorism? Secondly, should the PLF be considered a criminal organization, so that its members and those who set it up were guilty of conspiracy, quite apart from any other crime they might have committed? Thirdly, if the hijackers were indeed terrorists, could one invoke, as mitigating circumstances, the fact that they were fighting a war of national liberation?

Let us take a quick look at how the Court elucidated each question (as to the second of these, I shall also quote the decisions of the two Courts of Appeal, since on this point there was divergence of opinion between the first and the second set of decisions).

Was the hijacking of the Italian liner an act of terrorism?

This was a particularly thorny question. Was the taking over of the *Achille Lauro* and keeping its crew and passengers hostage for about three days (with the aggravating circumstance of the murder of one of the hostages) a crime as defined in Article 289 bis of the Italian criminal code: that is, a kidnapping of persons for terrorist ends? The Court thought it was. The judges believed that not only the three hijackers (the fourth, being under age at the time of the hijacking, was convicted by the Juvenile Court in Genoa, as I mentioned earlier), but also their sponsors and leaders (Abul Abbas and his two aides, Ez El Din Badrakhan – also spelt as Ozzudin Badraktan – and Ziad El Omar) were all guilty of this crime.

The crux of the problem was, naturally, the concept of the objectives of terrorism mentioned in Article 289 bis. The court understood this as follows: 'By terrorist objectives, we mean the determination to pursue a form of political struggle characterized by the systematic resort to particularly violent means, that is, to excessive, pitiless, gratuitous violence that shows an absolute contempt for the values that our legal system seeks to preserve, and such as to generate panic in the general public.' The Court then specified that the Italian criminal code requires that the *objective* of the action be that of terrorism; the action itself need not be violent: 'Thus,' the Court added, 'there can be crimes that are not at all violent whose objective is terrorism.' With this premise, it was easy for the judges to conclude that the Palestinians who planned or carried out the hijacking of the Italian liner had, as their objective, 'a method characterized by resort to particularly violent means, such as to generate panic in the general public'.

Can the PLF be considered to have committed conspiracy?

Like various other states, Italy punishes not only individual crimes, but also the fact of setting up a 'group' (*associazione*) with the intention of organizing criminal actions (robbery, drug peddling, exploitation of prostitutes, kidnapping people for ransom, etc.), or a political conspiracy against the state, or terrorism. The mere fact of promoting, setting up or organizing such a 'group', or even taking part in one, or giving help or sanctuary to one of the conspirators, is punished with penalties of varying length, which, however, are always extremely heavy. In the realm of political crimes, the Italian penal code punishes what is called 'armed band' (*banda armata*): this may be said to exist when a criminal 'group' acts to subvert the political order (it includes such acts as political or military spying and armed insurrection against the state, as well as attacks on 'constitutional bodies'). Furthermore, a group with subversive aims becomes an 'armed band' only if it fulfils certain requisites: it must include a number of members, its organization must be appropriate to its objectives, and it must possess arms.

As far as the judges in Genoa were concerned, the problem was whether the PLF could be termed an 'armed band' as defined in the Italian criminal code. In other words, should the hijackers (and their leaders) be punished only for the act of terrorism, or should they *also* be punished for having formed an 'armed band'? Obviously, this is not only a legal issue as to whether the accused should receive *longer* sentences if found guilty of this crime. The issue is above all political, moral and psychological: is the PLF a *group of criminals*, or is it a *legitimate* national liberation movement, pursuing acceptable objectives (the liberation of the Palestinian people), by means that are sometimes lawful, but which, sometimes, contravene the penal laws of various states?

The Court of Assizes (and the Juvenile Court, following on its heels) decided the PLF was not a *criminal organization*. The former Court observed that, in order to call a political group an 'armed band', one must distinguish between the *'contingent objective* pursued by a military type of armed organization, *in a specific moment* of its existence', and its 'essential objective, the one for which it was established, and for which it exists as an organization'. What matters, as the Court pointed out, is the 'essential objective'. If the group is to be termed an 'armed band', its 'essential objective' must be to commit a 'crime against the personality of the State', such as an armed insurrection or an attack on the 'constitutional bodies'. Even though, as the judges pointed out, an organization may be transformed, and change its objectives and structure, the vital clue to its real nature under criminal law is still the essential objective it is currently pursuing. The judges illustrated this concept with an example: suppose an ordinary criminal organization (such as a group of *mafiosi* or a band of robbers) possesses all the characteristics of an 'armed band' (see above), but its main objectives are to commit ordinary crimes and not to subvert the political order; it may so happen that its activities expand to such an extent that it engages in a civil war, 'directing all its activities and organization to this end, and no longer trying merely to acquire illicit profits for its members'. In this case a group committing ordinary crimes is transformed into a subversive group. What really matters for this purpose is whether that criminal group's essential objective has become political subversion, and that the whole organization has been oriented towards that aim. If, after the 'transformation', the group commits *ordinary crimes* (by robbing a bank, for example), it must nevertheless be considered a subversive *political* organization, in other words an 'armed band'.

However, in the case of the *Achille Lauro* – the Court warned – *exactly the reverse* was true. The PLF's 'essential' or 'institutional objective' was the liberation of Palestine by political and military means; this objective bore no comparison to that of an 'armed band', which is to subvert the political order of the Italian state. On to this 'essential objective' was grafted, as it were, the '*contingent objective*' of *one single action*: the hijacking of the Italian ship. The specific aim of the hijacking was to commit a crime 'against the State'. Since under Italian law, what matters is the 'essential objective', the PLF as such could not be considered a subversive political organization. As the Court put it:

It is true that this politico-military organization [the PLF] possesses all the basic features of an armed band: a number of adherents, an inner hierarchical structure of a military type, possession of arms. But, these features are essential to the organization's main objective: to help return the Palestinians to their country of origin. These adherents have coalesced around that objective, to achieve it they created that structure, bought those arms, carried out those actions – of a military, terrorist or political nature – that the Front thought necessary, in diverse situations and according to its ideology and strategic vision of things. There is no evidence that that objective ever changed.

In a nutshell, the Court considered that, under Italian law, only armed groups set up with the specific purpose of subverting, or at least of hitting out at, Italy's political and constitutional system, were to be considered subversive criminal groups. An organized band of armed men, set up to fight *against a foreign country* (e.g. the IRA, the Basque armed groups, the Armenians, the Kurds, etc.), cannot be considered an 'armed band'. Should it commit crimes on Italian territory, against Italian nationals or Italian possessions, it can be punished, but *only for these crimes*. In other words, under Italian criminal law these groups, so long as they do not injure Italian 'interests', are regarded as, if not actually legitimate, at least not illegal.

On this point, Italian criminal law may seem rather 'nationalistic' and insensitive to international cooperation in the fight against terrorism. Some might even object that Italy is considering itself a secluded island, forgetting how armed violence has branched out on an international plane, showing scant interest in the vicissitudes of other states and concentrating its efforts on preserving its own political and social structure by punishing anyone who threatens its existence.

In my opinion, in spite of its undoubtedly nationalistic 'flavour' which cannot but arouse serious objections, by and large the Court's interpretation – or, to be more accurate, its gist – is in line with current trends in the international community, as reflected in its rules and principles. In other words, in choosing to examine the standing of the PLO and its various inner factions from the point of view of Italian domestic law, the Court formed an appraisal very similar to that which results from the rules governing the international community today. The international community grants limited international personality to any national liberation movement possessing certain features (an effective organization and international legitimacy due to its having been recognized by a considerable number of states or intergovernmental organizations, such as the United Nations, the Organization of African Unity, or the League of Arab States).

This means, above all, that certain national liberation movements are accepted by the international community as the counterparts – at least to a certain extent – of sovereign states, the real protagonists in international affairs. Naturally, this is so only if the national liberation movement's 'apparatus' is not to be considered a 'criminal organization', at least in its international relations (even though under the domestic law of the state against which it is fighting, together with that of some other states, it will inevitably be considered criminal). As a consequence of its acquiring international legal personality, the national liberation movement's bodies and agencies are, from certain points of view, equated with state bodies: for instance, when they enter into international agreements, or when they send diplomatic 'missions', or take part in the meetings of intergovernmental organizations, or participate in 'legitimate' acts of war against the state they are fighting. Accordingly, whenever they undertake such actions, the organs of a national liberation movement can invoke the international rule whereby a foreign state has no jurisdiction over the actions of individuals acting in their official capacity as state agents.

Thus, a PLO leader is not held personally responsible, and cannot be brought before the courts of a state for acts that he performed for, and in the name of, the PLO – on condition that these acts are among those 'protected' by international law (namely those which I have just referred to). It follows that 'third states', such as Italy, that have recognized or in some way admitted the legitimacy of a national liberation movement, cannot, by that very fact, regard it as a 'criminal organization'. Further, they should attribute the acts of its leaders, or agents, only to the organization itself. On the other hand, they are authorized to punish any act that international law does not regard as legitimate: for instance, acts of terrorism, or acts of war that violate international rules on the conduct of hostilities, such as maltreating or killing prisoners of war, or bombing 'protected buildings' such as hospitals, churches, etc.

Since the PLO and its various factions are among the few national liberation movements whose international legitimacy has been recognized by many states in the world community, it was not possible to treat the PLO as such, or one of its factions, as a criminal organization. Nevertheless, the hijacking of the *Achille Lauro* was undoubtedly a crime and its instigators and perpetrators were, accordingly, to be punished for it. It follows that Abul Abbas' statement, during an interview in April 1987, that he could go to Italy and be treated as one of the PLO's 'ministers' (in other words, was not subject to Italian criminal jurisdiction), has *no foundation whatsoever*, either in Italian law or in international law. In my opinion, international law points to the same conclusions as those drawn by the Genoese court, which reached this result by a perspicacious application of Italian criminal law.

The 'armed band' issue in the Courts of Appeal

After my long digression on international law, I must return to the Courts' decisions. Why did the conclusions of the two Courts of Appeal differ from those of the two Courts at first instance as to whether the PLF was to be held guilty of constituting an 'armed band'? The two Courts of Appeal adopted an interpretation that fell between the interpretation of the Court of Assizes and that advanced by the public prosecutor for Genoa in his appeal against the judgment of the Juvenile Court. He stated that, on the whole, the PLF should be regarded as an 'armed band', that is, as 'an international terrorist organization'. His submission was that an 'armed unit' is an 'armed band' when its objectives are subversive, even if these are 'instrumental to the final aims' of the unit. He added that, in any case, at least the group that had organized the hijacking should be considered an 'armed band': since the group had the 'characteristic stability and permanence' necessary to prove the 'minimal hypothesis that an armed band had been set up in Genoa'.

It is precisely this 'minimal hypothesis' that was accepted by the two Appellate Courts. They held that *it was not the PLF*, but the *tiny nucleus* that conceived, planned, directed and carried out the hijacking that had formed an 'armed band'. Let me take a step back and remind the reader that this interpretation of the facts had already been rejected by both the Court of Assizes and the Juvenile Court. They had held that the armed nucleus set up to hijack the *Achille Lauro* possessed neither 'the necessary characteristics of autonomy from its parent-body [the PLF] nor stability and permanence'. Moreover, according to Italian criminal law, an 'armed band' cannot be a 'sectorial organism', as the nucleus undoubtedly was. This was precisely the holding that the two Appellate Courts reversed. They advanced three arguments to support their view.

First, an 'armed band' can easily be formed by a *sectorial organism* acting as a separate 'compartment':

in the day to day reality of criminal phenomena [the 'armed band' is a] group that does, by definition, distribute duties, possess arms, and – obviously – pursue a fundamental aim; yet [it] does not act according to rigid rules of behaviour, to rules of coherence, or with respect for the 'democratic' principle of immediately transmitting to its members the operational policies of its Command; instead, it is characterized by elastic and opportunist schemes of behaviour, that are not those of a lawful association with legal personality. (Decision of the Appellate Court of Assizes)

The second argument refers not to the structure of an armed nucleus, but to its objectives. According to the Courts of Appeal, the *subversive aims* of an armed group can be *instrumental* with regard to its main objectives: as the Appeal Section for the Juvenile Court observed – in rather convoluted terms –

the danger posed by the group to the interests protected by law is the same, whether or not the subversive aims of the group are principal or incidental. In other words, it [the danger] exists as soon as the armed group sets its course for a head on collision with the Law . . . it is in the very moment that the group chooses its objectives (whether or not they are its only, or final, aims) that it becomes a dangerous group.

The third argument revolved around the activities and 'permanence' of the criminal armed nucleus. According to the Courts of Appeal, the nucleus can be an 'armed band' even if it is set up *for a specific action* and is *disbanded* once the action itself had been carried out.

It is not my intention – nor is it within my province – to say whether these arguments are sound under Italian criminal law. I shall merely remark that the two Courts of Appeal were very skilful in sailing safely between Scylla and Charybdis: they avoided giving, in their judgment, too 'nationalistic' or too 'biased' an interpretation of the concept of 'armed band'; they also avoided accusing the whole PLF – let alone the PLO – of being a criminal organization, which would probably have been excessive in the circumstances. Thus the two Courts of Appeal reached a decision – like the other two courts before them – *that did not conflict with international law*. Indeed, international law does not deny that a state can legitimately consider the armed nucleus or faction of a national liberation movement a criminal organization that plans and carries out terrorist actions more or less systematically. Naturally, such an 'accusation' or assessment does not necessarily involve the whole movement, so long as the latter pursues legitimate political objectives, by dint of activities that have been 'approved' as legitimate by most of the members of the international community.

At this point, let us return to the judgment of the Court of Assizes to see what decision it reached on the issue of mitigating circumstances.

Were there any mitigating circumstances for the hijackers?

Besides pleading that the PLF should not be accused of being a criminal organization, the defence counsel argued that the political ideals of the accused constituted mitigating circumstances. They claimed that the Palestinians had been inspired by 'high moral and social values'. Quite rightly, the Court rejected this plea: such mitigating circumstances could not be taken into account for terrorist crimes. This, the Court added, was because 'in the present state of our country's political and social set up . . . the use of terrorism, as a form of political struggle, seems contrary to ordinary people's moral conscience, whatever the ultimate objectives of that struggle.' On the other hand, the Court felt that it could take into account the so-called general mitigating circumstances applying to the three hijackers: that is, those circumstances relating to 'the personality of the criminal or to the objective or subjective facts surrounding the crime'. On this point, the judges remarked that they must take into consideration the social and family situation of the three hijackers:

Al Assadi, Al Molqi, Fataier were all born in those refugee camps in which the problems besetting the Palestinian people take on violent hues; they grew up – hardly by choice – in an atmosphere of often indiscriminate violence; because of the indifference of others to their problems, they were led to believe that these problems could only be solved by the use of arms. This was the breeding ground for their unfortunate actions: at an age when children usually have other interests, the three men learned to use deadly weapons (both Fataier and Al Molqi joined Palestinian armed organizations at the age of nine; Al Assadi did likewise at eleven); later, all three spent their adolescence and the earliest years of their youth moving from one military camp to another, each one some distance from the next and always far from the refugee camps where their families lived, before ending up in a 'suicide unit' (joining it when very young and knowing full well what this implied).

Once again, the Genoese judges' appraisal was balanced and objective: they took into account the social context and the conditions in which the hijackers had lived, without going so far as to attribute 'special' social and moral values to the Palestinians. The hijacking and murder were serious terrorist crimes, but it was humane and just not to overlook the historical circumstances which led to them.

8

The Lessons of
the *Achille Lauro* Affair

I have reached the end of my examination of the various episodes in an affair that revealed so much about relations between states and the impact of terrorism on governments. I fear I have failed to clarify, let alone solve, many problems, leaving instead a trail of new questions in my wake. Perhaps I may have disappointed my reader, like the inquiring magistrate in one of Maupassant's short stories, who, having regaled his audience with a blood-curdling story full of enigmas, then refused to solve the mystery and was reproached for leaving his listeners 'without explanation nor ending'. Let me hasten to say that it is hard to illuminate episodes as complex and multifaceted as those of the *Achille Lauro* affair except through a series of scattered close-ups. Besides, unlike the French magistrate, I shall at least try to draw some conclusions and give the reader a kind of epilogue, in which I intend to enumerate the lessons I feel ought to be drawn from the dramatic events of that one week.

VIOLENCE OR DIPLOMATIC NEGOTIATION THROUGH LAW: TWO ALTERNATIVES

One of today's most penetrating observers of the international scene, Raymond Aron, has argued that, in essence, relations between states can be broken down into those conducted by 'ambassadors' and those conducted by 'soldiers'. He thus sums up the two fundamental approaches of states: the wielding of peaceful tools of diplomatic negotiation, and the brandishing of threats and armed violence. These two approaches are not mutually exclusive, rather they complement one another; in point of fact, states switch from one to the other, the 'ambassador' at times prevailing over the 'soldier' and vice versa.

Generally speaking, this analysis holds true both from an historical and a political point of view. However, a lawyer, like myself, is trained to use the 'tablets of the law' as his starting point; thus, I cannot help asking myself whether the principles embodied in current international law favour the 'soldier' or the 'ambassador'. (Here, I must explain to any reader who is tired of my constant reliance upon value judgements, that I do not agree with the well-known French historian, Marc Bloch, who asserted that a scholar should merely comprehend, whereas a judge should comprehend and evaluate, condemn or acquit, according to a predetermined scale of values. His theory is valid in the case of historians and other experts in the social sciences, but not in the case of legal scholars, at least not those whom Hitler so despised, as I recalled in my Foreword. A legal scholar must not only comprehend, but must also assess on the basis of a given set of values; to be sure, not his personal values, but those of his national legal system – or, in the case of international lawyers, the values of the world community.)

Now, I feel that there are sufficient – relatively objective – points of reference in the international community to allow us to appraise the specific aims of states. Thus, the rules governing international relations clearly *insist* that the tools of diplomacy should always be used: 'soldiers' should appear on the scene only in exceptional circumstances, when no practical or lawful alternative exists.

I feel it is right to ask ourselves which of the states involved in the *Achille Lauro* affair put forward their 'ambassador' to deal with the hijacking and which preferred to use only their 'soldiers'. In other words, which states respected the general dictates of international law, and which preferred to go their own way.

As we have seen in the preceding pages, one state (the USA) chose the military option, whereas the other two (Italy and Egypt) settled for patient, if exhausting, negotiation. From the very beginning, the United States told Craxi it was 'completely averse to taking part in any form of negotiation'; it then went on to violate the sovereign rights of both Egypt and Italy and, worse still, used force against Egypt in a way that was totally unjustified under international law.

However, although Egypt and Italy chose to negotiate, this does not mean *these two states respected the dictates of law scrupulously*. As Machiavelli remarked: 'only rarely do men know how to be totally bad or totally good.' As I have already noted, Egypt did not respect the 1979 Convention on the Taking of Hostages *vis-à-vis* the United States, while in the last phase of the affair Italy failed to respect its 1983 extradition treaty with the United States.

Let me hasten to add that I am not so naive as to consider respect for the law a supreme value to which everything should be sacrificed. States are such complex mechanisms and their interests so multifaceted that they cannot behave like knights in search of the Holy Grail, for whom law and justice were supreme. As all lawyers know, though laymen perhaps do not, legal rules are not mythical imperatives, but merely earthly standards of behaviour. By embodying certain sets of values, they create specific expectations in the various 'actors' in the community. These rules serve as reminders: should we fail to respect their dictates, we can expect the censure of others (entailing a trial, a sentence, a fine, public reproof, and so on, according to the sophistication of the sanctioning mechanism); should we respect these rules, although we may not receive any applause, we shall at least have behaved as others expected (and hoped) we would.

Thus, when we say a state has observed or violated international law, what we mean is that it has, or has not, respected those values it had previously (even if tacitly) accepted. If its behaviour was not in accordance with the expectations of other states, it will incur their 'reprobation'. International rules – like any other form of law – resemble Spinoza's 'foundations of the State'; he characterized these foundations as 'the king's *eternal* decrees' that must be respected by his ministers even when this would entail a refusal to obey the king's *specific* commands. To illustrate his point, Spinoza recalled how Ulysses made his companions tie him to the mast so as to resist the sirens' song, insisting that they should not free him whatever might happen; and, fortunately, they paid no heed when, bewitched by the sirens' singing, he ordered his companions to untie him. Similarly, present-day international rules are the 'ties' – some looser than others – by which states prevent themselves from being seduced by nationalism and violence.

Unfortunately, as we all know, the mechanisms for enforcing sanctions in the international community are extremely faulty. Thus, it can seem otiose to ask whether, by harking to the sirens' song, a state has committed a breach of international law. That is why I feel that any evaluation of a state's behaviour should, from the very beginning, be conducted along two separate lines. The first is *ethical* and *political*: public opinion (and this includes the whole international community and all those private citizens who follow international affairs with interest and trepidation) must be informed when a state has committed a breach of given rules of the international 'code of conduct' that it had previously accepted. The second line of inquiry is mainly *cognitive*. It consists in asking why a state violated, or observed, the law on a certain occasion. What were the non-legal reasons for its doing so? Were they political, strategic or psychological? Did it have other, reasonable alternatives?

In the preceding chapters of this book (especially chapters 4, 5 and 6) I have tried to give an answer to these questions in the case of the *Achille Lauro* affair.

THE COSTS AND BENEFITS OF OBSERVING THE LAW

I should now like to deal with the following question: *who paid the highest price, those who observed or those who violated the basic legal principles forbidding resort to force?*

In my opinion, by disregarding the fundamental principles of international law, the United States sailed into a sea of political and diplomatic troubles. Not only did it fail to achieve its purpose (the capture and trial of the hijackers), it also antagonized and deeply offended two allies, one a member of NATO.

Further, with the exception of Israel, the reaction of other states was negative. These states fear the consequences of the *precedent* set by the Americans just as strongly as do Egypt and Italy. By resorting to force, the United States fell into the trap of *'hijacking' the hijackers*. They did so in pursuance of US strategy in matters of terrorism, which, as we have seen, rests on an (at times excessive) readiness to take coercive measures affecting other states. It should be mentioned in this connection that there are some signs that US policy may be changing. The recent decision of the US District Court for the District of Columbia in *USA v Fawaz Yunis* (12 February 1988) perhaps points in the direction of a greater reliance on peaceful means of dealing with terrorists. The case involved a Lebanese alleged to have hijacked a Jordanian aircraft (carrying a number of US nationals), who was, in effect, lured to international waters and there arrested and taken to the United States for trial under the relevant American anti-terrorist legislation. Of course, an element of coercion was involved here as well, but not against another state – not, in other words, such as would disturb international relations.

But let us return to the American conduct during the *Achille Lauro* affair. The interception was described by the PLO representative in the UN Security Council as a form of 'official terrorism' and then by President Mubarak as an 'act of piracy . . . without precedent in any international code or law'.

And indeed, in a few hours the United States managed to destroy the huge consensus that had been mounting since the hijacking of the Italian liner, and which had been officially expressed in the solemn declaration made by the President of the Security Council in the name of all fifteen members on 9 October. In short, the United States' breach of the law was 'far from profitable' in political and diplomatic terms, as well as from the point of view of the Americans' immediate purposes.

Some readers may object that the United States' intention was to 'warn' certain states (Libya, Syria, Iran) and various terrorist organizations that any future terrorist action of similar gravity would provoke a military response. There is no doubt that this was indeed one of the reasons behind the Americans' decision to use force. But did it 'pay off' in political and diplomatic terms? All those who sponsor, direct, support, or carry out acts of terrorism certainly received 'due warning'. But in my opinion the price paid for the warning was too high. Now any other state (including the other superpower, which refrained from condemning or protesting formally against the American gesture) knows it can cite the American precedent to justify resort to force on similar occasions. Thus, the floating mine laid by the Americans on the high seas of international affairs could have devastating effects that will outweigh by far any 'positive' results.

As regards Italy and Egypt, on the whole they applied one of Machiavelli's most famous maxims (that the 'enemy should be either cajoled or extinguished'), with a marked preference for cajoling. However, to the extent that they too showed little respect for the law, their actions also did not pay off.

When Egypt failed to abide by the 1979 Convention on the Taking of Hostages – due, probably, to the difficult state of its home affairs that forced it to deal with the PLO and extremist Egyptian groups with 'kid gloves' – it provoked the Americans' use of force, thereby increasing tension at home and risking the fall of the Mubarak Government. Its violation of international law only paid off in part. As for Italy, the ambiguity of its behaviour during negotiations for the safe-conduct agreement was probably determined by its desire to end the hijacking and avoid any deterioration in the international crisis that might endanger the lives of the hostages. Its failure to apply the 1983 treaty with the United States did 'pay off' in terms of policy and diplomatic relations. That is, it was successful in avoiding future terrorist attacks by the PLF in Italy, in obtaining the release of the Italian liner, and in helping to preserve the stability of the Mubarak regime. At the same time, its action had adverse effects at home, where tension between the five parties of the coalition increased, and also damaged its relations with the United States. In more general terms, it cast a shadow over the Italian Government's firm resolve to punish terrorists *at all levels*.

LONG-TERM, MEDIUM-TERM AND SHORT-TERM
FOREIGN POLICY OBJECTIVES

Let us now see whether the states involved in the *Achille Lauro* affair, especially the United States and Italy, pursued long-term, medium-term or short-term foreign policy objectives.

At the beginning of the crisis, the United States merely applied the policy it had already devised for cases of terrorism, a policy determined by what it considered to be its vital interests and by its political philosophy (see chapter 5). I should add that this was based on one of the tenets of American foreign policy: a preference for *order and stability*, as opposed to social, political and institutional change. In the United States terrorism is seen as a violent rift in the established order; no account is taken of the fact that it may *also* reflect a desire for *social change*, innovation and the adaptation of international relations to changing needs, even when, alas, these are expressed in such perverted and destructive ways.

When the United States decided to eschew any form of negotiation, it exposed itself to two separate criticisms. As we now know, its attitude of intransigence towards the Palestinian hijackers was a façade, since the Reagan administration was in fact negotiating with Iran for the release of US hostages. Furthermore, its intransigence reflected short-term considerations, which surfaced as soon as it was known that the hijackers were threatening the lives of American citizens. The interception of the Egyptian aircraft was merely the result of a foreign policy determined more by the pressure of public opinion than by a long-term view. The American use of force jeopardized its good relations with a vital ally in the Middle East, and even threatened to topple the regime of that ally. Moreover, its action set a dangerous precedent and created a 'model of behaviour' that would be easy to follow, and was indeed imitated almost at once by Israel, thereby forcing the United States to 'adjust' its legal approach to the use of force; an adjustment that has proved to be even more dangerous for the international community than the wavering justifications advanced by the Americans for having intercepted the Egyptian aircraft.

And yet, we should not be surprised that the United States acted on this occasion, as on similar ones, on the basis of short-term considerations. This approach was recently given a theoretical basis by an American political scientist (Richard H. Shultz Jr) in his analysis of the United States' struggle against terrorism. His general argument was that one of the tenets of US foreign policy since World War II is the principle that 'in an anarchic system, each state must put concern for its short-term interests above concern for long-term absolute gain or change.'

Let us now turn to Italy. Although it had a precise short-term objective (the release of the hostages without bloodshed), the Italian Government's policy was, on the whole, more far-sighted: it wanted to achieve a *peaceful* end to the crisis (with military intervention only as a last resort); and at the same time sought to preserve *good relations* with all the main actors in the Mediterranean area (including the PLO), and to bolster the *stability* of the Egyptian Government. All this did not prevent it from issuing a firm condemnation of terrorism and of all its pernicious consequences. One can criticize the behaviour of the Italian Government at the conclusion of the safe-conduct agreement as ambiguous (but not cowardly, as some have called it). Apart from this, even the government's refusal to grant the Americans' requests, and the eventual breach of the extradition treaty with the United States that led to such tension between the two countries, seem to have been the result of a *basic* foreign policy choice: Italy was seeking to be increasingly independent of its 'Big Brother', as well as strengthening its future role in the Mediterranean area. Both these points were reiterated by Craxi in his speech to the Senate on 3 March 1987, when he described the three cornerstones of his government's foreign policy as: 'a strong sense of independence', 'great loyalty towards our allies' and 'a firm defence of human rights and the rights of people'. Let me add that it was precisely these broad policies that enabled the government not to be swayed – at least to no great extent – by the pressure of public opinion at home, or by tension within the five-party coalition.

It is instructive to compare Italy's 'reaction' with that of Mussolini in 1923, after the terrorist attack on General Tellini and his men at Jannina in Greece, which I mentioned earlier. In 1923, Italy had no hesitation in resorting to force and bombed Corfu, because Greece (held responsible by Mussolini) had not immediately complied with Italy's exorbitant requests. Today, Italy's attitude is very different, and reflects the new ideals that inspire the international community (and the Italian Constitution). Herein lies the strength of Italy's position throughout the *Achille Lauro* affair: its behaviour was, in the main, consonant with the aims of the United Nations Charter – that is, with the ideals that ought to inspire the foreign policy of all states.

POSITIVE AND NEGATIVE PEACE

We have seen that in the *Achille Lauro* affair the United States acted on the basis of short-term considerations while Italy acted, in general, on the basis of slightly longer-term – say, 'medium-term' – considerations. This appears to reflect a pattern as regards counter-terrorist response whereby short-term considerations are pursued with force, while medium-term considerations are pursued by peaceful means (negotiation, conclusion of agreements etc.). I shall suggest below a third type of response which in my view satisfies long-term objectives.

But first, let us consider in turn the efficacy of each of these types of response in terms of their respective contributions to the elimination of terrorism. The coercive response, although actually ineffective in the *Achille Lauro* affair, may sometimes yield immediate *short-term* gains and one can appreciate that for this reason it often seems attractive: terrorists may be killed or captured before they can carry out, or complete, terrorist attacks. No time is 'wasted' during which innocent lives could be lost. And yet these immediate benefits are really a mirage, for beyond them lies a vast whirlpool of spiralling violence. Once the hijackers are themselves hijacked, who knows but that those who hijack the hijackers will not also be hijacked? Thus, the hijack of hijackers becomes not the end of hijacking but the beginning of new hijacking. Violence, as the old saying goes, only ever begets more violence.

What of the peaceful responses? As Italy's conduct during the *Achille Lauro* affair showed, these can be effective responses in the *medium-term*. Although it takes time and patience to negotiate, to cooperate, to set in motion judicial procedures, ultimately those who commit terrorist crimes are put in gaol and, on the whole, violence and dangerous diplomatic tensions are avoided. Had Italy been prepared to carry out its treaty obligations to the full (by complying with the United States' extradition request or at least granting the United States time to complete its extradition application), its medium-term objectives would have been even more effectively served, at least in respect of Abul Abbas. And yet, I do not believe that ultimately extradition treaties and treaties on cooperation in dealing with hostage-takers and the like really provide a *long-term* solution to the problem of terrorism.

At this point I wish to refer to the concepts of 'positive' and 'negative' peace enunciated by the eminent peace-researcher, Johan Galtung. In a nutshell 'negative peace', in Galtung's conception, is the mere absence of armed conflict, whereas 'positive peace' is the absence of structural violence or social injustices of various types. As I have indicated, the coercive forms of response to terrorism are, in reality, incitements to further violence and can achieve neither kind of peace. So far as the 'peaceful' forms of response – negotiations, conclusion and implementation of treaties etc. – are concerned, it seems to me that the most these can achieve is 'negative peace', a situation where no blood is spilled, no shots are fired. Negative peace is obviously better than no peace at all but in my view the real key to suppressing terrorism in a lasting way lies in pursuing 'positive peace'.

By this I mean that, in addition to dealing (in a strictly peaceful way) with each terrorist incident *ad hoc* as it arises and taking action to deter or forestall future specific terrorist attacks, it is imperative that efforts also be turned towards identifying and eliminating the root causes of terrorist activity. This is the third kind of response – the long-term response – I mentioned earlier. Although this response is apt to be overlooked, a large measure of support for it already exists. In particular, the two most recent General Assembly resolutions on terrorism (those in 1985 and 1987) urge states to 'contribute to the progressive elimination of the causes underlying international terrorism and to pay special attention to all situations, including, *inter alia*, colonialism, racism and situations involving mass and flagrant violations of human rights and fundamental freedoms and those involving alien occupation, that may give rise to international terrorism and may endanger international peace and security'. Here we find reference to some elements of structural violence believed by the General Assembly to stand in the way of the lasting elimination of terrorism. The problem was also eloquently highlighted by the Ghanaian representative in the Security Council in the debate following the Israeli interception of a

Libyan aircraft in February 1986. He stated: '. . . the international community, including the [Security] Council, must summon the necessary political will to delve into the reasons why the frustrations of the dispossessed are vented in this manner. A glib condemnation of terrorism alone, without a specific and impartial study of its origins will not, we are afraid, eradicate the phenomenon.'

It is immediately obvious that the long-term goal of establishing a true, 'positive' peace – and with it, putting behind us all terrorist activity – cannot be achieved by endless agreements between states. Of course, these will remain necessary in the interim for dealing with outbreaks of terrorism and can to a degree assist in alleviating some elements of structural violence, particularly those mentioned in the General Assembly resolutions referred to above. This point was made by the American delegate to the UN General Assembly's Sixth Committee in the debates concerning the 1987 resolution on terrorism to which I have just referred. He stated that, while 'there was a need to eliminate the underlying causes of terrorism . . . it would be both illogical and contrary to United Nations practice to condition the taking of measures to combat terrorism on the elimination of its causes.' However, there are certainly many elements of structural violence which states either have a vested interest in maintaining or in any event (in the present international system of sovereign states) cannot be compelled to remove. It follows that any attempt to examine and tackle the causes of terrorism must be conducted also at the level of individuals and non-state groups.

This theory, that one should endeavour to analyse and try to remove the causes that give rise to terrorism, may indeed seem too abstract and vague. Admittedly it requires great patience and tenacity if it is to be put into practice, and would bear fruit only after a very long time. It also requires, in the meantime, a degree of vigilance to ensure that the study of the causes of terrorism is not turned into an excercise in rationalizing, and ultimately justifying, terrorism. And, of course, even after the causes appear to have been removed, one must expect that dangerous hotbeds of political violence will remain. Human aspirations and actions can take unpredictable turns, and, as already discussed, are often irrational and unconnected to 'objective' factors. However, in setting our sights – far and high – on 'positive peace', we will have at least gone some way towards reducing the prospects for terrorist activity.

THE ROLE PLAYED BY NATIONAL JUDGES IN TRANSNATIONAL AFFAIRS

Elsewhere I have tried to show how the exposure of municipal courts to international issues is always beneficial (see my book on *Violence and Law in the Modern Age*, 1988). Fearing that their mutual relations might suffer, national governments often hesitate before taking action against other states, especially if this involves accusing the other state of having violated the rights of individuals. In cases such as these, foreign offices prefer to shelve the issue, or, if it cannot be avoided, to reach a solution via secret negotiation, often to the detriment of the individuals concerned. It is precisely in these cases that municipal courts can compensate for the tardiness or deficiencies of the executive, and ensure that justice prevails.

In the *Achille Lauro* affair, the judges played a useful role. However, one must draw a distinction between what the judges were called upon to do in one phase of the affair, and what the courts decided after the affair was over.

The first phase started when the Egyptian plane was forced to land at a NATO airbase in Italy. The two public prosecutors in Genoa and Syracuse (who, like all Italian public prosecutors, are members of the judiciary) were called in, both to question the four hijackers, and to give an opinion on the 'interim measures' to be adopted with regard to Abul Abbas. At the same time, three high-ranking officials of the Ministry of Justice (again members of the judiciary) gave their opinion on the legal basis for the American request for the 'provisional arrest' of the Palestinian leader. Thus, in this phase the judges can be said to have played a 'supporting role' to the executive. It was suggested by the American authorities that the Italian judges merely furnished their government with a formal pretext for allowing Abul Abbas to go free; the Americans also felt the Italian judges had been influenced more by 'reasons of state' than by those of justice. It is my view, however – both because the Italian judiciary is totally independent and because the opinion came not from a single judge, but from the judges of Genoa, Rome and Syracuse – that the Americans' criticisms are, on the whole, without foundation. It cannot, however, be denied that the opinions expressed by these judges were useful to the government in this stage of negotiations and decisions, especially with regard to its policy towards Egypt.

The role played by the Italian judges in the second phase were even more important. The Genoese courts did not at this stage have to justify any shortcomings or failures on the part of the government: their task was to *settle* an issue that fell under their jurisdiction as a result of the action by the executive and after the United States had intercepted the Egyptian aircraft. They were not called upon to act with courage and initiative, as certain municipal courts have done in the past in defying government entities that had failed to defend, or had even violated, human rights. None the less, they did make an important contribution on two counts: first, they made sure that *justice was done* and the guilty parties duly punished; secondly, they were able to *throw new light* on the whole affair.

As to the first point, it is obvious that cases of transnational terrorism are best dealt with by municipal courts, since the appropriate international courts do not exist. It is always preferable that the guilt or innocence of an alleged terrorist be evaluated by the judiciary rather than by the executive.

As far as the second point is concerned, the impartiality and thoroughness of municipal courts, as well as their powers and rigorous procedure for obtaining evidence, enable them to throw light on numerous aspects of terrorist crimes. By so doing, the courts can help politicians, diplomats, the military and legal scholars to gain a better understanding of terrorist actions and the various contributing factors that determine their success or failure. This is precisely what happened in the *Achille Lauro* episode (see chapter 7): the Genoa Court of Assizes was of enormous help in clarifying several cryptic episodes in the hijacking affair.

I should add that, although the Court chose to examine the facts in the light of domestic law, its analysis respected the various requirements of international law. Thus, though the Court condemned terrorism, it did not condemn the Palestinian organization that is fighting for the freedom of its people. In the end, the Court's decision was entirely in line with the Italian Government's foreign policy, despite its independence and full autonomy from the executive. As we saw earlier (chapter 7), the two Courts of Appeal adopted a slightly different attitude; but even their decisions did not conflict with the political and diplomatic imperatives of the international community.

THE NEFARIOUS CONSEQUENCES OF TERRORISM

The *Achille Lauro* affair taught us another lesson: *terrorism has a profoundly adverse impact on the international community.*

First and foremost for the obvious reason that it poses a constant threat to the lives of innocent people. Terrorism – at least in the form often used by national liberation movements – has another extremely pernicious side to it: it is inspired by ideologies *tainted with racism*. Once the hijackers took over the *Achille Lauro* (chapter 3), they picked out not only the American and British citizens, but also all those who were Jewish, whatever their nationality. Their choice of Leon Klinghoffer as their first victim has prompted one commentator (F. Gerardi) to say that probably none of these young Palestinians realized that 'their horrible criterion for selecting the hostages [was] identical to that which led to the holocaust

in the Nazi concentration camps.' So racist a choice was hardly
new, as Shimon Peres, the then Israeli Prime Minister,
pointed out on 11 October 1985. The same had occurred on
the TWA plane, hijacked on 13 June 1985, when the terrorists
'separated Jews from non-Jews, even though there had been
no Israelis on board. And on the [Air France] plane [hijacked]
to Entebbe [in 1976] they did likewise.'

Clearly, some movements that resort to terrorism reintroduce
into the international community those racist ideologies that
should have disappeared forever, or so we all had hoped,
after having been unanimously condemned. These same
movements warmly support egalitarian ideologies (such as the
prohibition of all forms of discrimination based on the colour
of a person's skin); yet, while they struggle for the perfectly
just ideals of freeing oppressed peoples and winning back their
homeland or a national territory of their own, they taint their
propaganda with poison, whose odious and insidious nature
cannot fail to be recognized even by those who, in principle,
support these national liberation movements.

Further, terrorism has a negative impact on the international
community because it subverts the 'rules of the game'
accepted by all sovereign states. States are quite accustomed to
defending themselves from violence perpetrated by other
states, or by insurgents operating from within other states,
and have set up a body of rules to deal with such occurrences.
When, in the past, individuals (the pirates *juris gentium*)
disturbed international relations, sovereign states agreed to
take it upon themselves to use force against these subversives.
Terrorism has introduced an explosive new element into this
order. Although sovereign states have applied international
instruments to the phenomenon (the various multilateral
treaties for the arrest, punishment or extradition of terrorists),
these have proved inadequate. Terrorism upsets the rules of
the game, because it leads some states (in our case, the United
States) to commit glaring breaches of these fundamental
principles on the use of force, while inducing others (in this
case, Egypt and Italy) to breach specific treaties, as well as to

use subterfuge and other expedients. *Negotiation*, which should always be the preferred way out of a crisis, can falter and fail, and even states that usually choose peaceful solutions can be induced to make ambiguous concessions or accept dubious compromises. If states find themselves caught between the alternatives of 'cajoling' and 'extinguishing' the terrorists, this is because the odious phenomenon has such tremendous powers of subversion: as I have indicated, governments would do well to apply their energies to the elimination of the *causes* of terrorism as soon as possible.

Let me add one other consideration. In the long run, the 'losers' of terrorism are not only sovereign states, but those movements that try to set themselves up as the valid counterparts of the traditional subjects of the international community. The *Achille Lauro* hijacking upset the PLO no less than the various states involved in the affair. The very fact that the hijacking was carried out shows scant regard for the PLO's own 'Revolutionary Penal Code', to which I referred in chapter 4. Further, although a number of states, especially Egypt and Italy, kept in constant touch with the Organization, treating it as a partner on equal terms (with Italy even considering requesting – or actually requesting – the PLO to extradite the hijackers), yet, from the very beginning, the PLO proved to have more than one voice, and nothing could later dissipate the impression of ambiguity it had created. The PLO immediately denied it had had anything to do with the hijacking, condemning it in harsh terms. However, it then sent Abul Abbas himself to 'negotiate' with the hijackers: that is, the man who had thought up and planned the act of terrorism and, in any case, the man who was the hijackers' leader. Besides, only recently, Abul Abbas told the press that he had not been disowned by the leaders of the PLO for the hijacking of the Italian liner, let alone 'punished' in accordance with the Revolutionary Penal Code. His only 'constraint' has been that he has had to keep up the pretence that the Palestinians' original objective had been to attack the Israeli port of Ashdod; this lie has political and psychological motives, as I tried to explain in chapter 7. It is hardly surprising then, that the Italian Foreign Minister, Giulio Andreotti, whom no one could accuse of prejudice or hostility towards the PLO, should recently have voiced his bewilderment at Arafat's behaviour.

Thus, the whole *Achille Lauro* incident has pointed to a sad truth: the most credible national liberation movement and the one most widely 'recognized' by the international community, *has proved unsuccessful at standing as a valid counterpart for sovereign states*, because it is rent by bitter rivalries, its leaders' action and declarations are ambiguous, and it is further weakened by the lack of a national territory or government. Thus, terrorism has proved to be a losing card even for the most 'accepted' non-state 'player' on the international scene.

DOES THE INTERNATIONAL COMMUNITY HAVE THE TOOLS TO COMBAT TERRORISM?

In view of what happened over the hijacking of the *Achille Lauro*, let us now ask ourselves whether the rules, procedures and strategies that states have developed have proved useful and effective in dealing with terrorism.

What took place after the Italian liner had been hijacked shows how the international community has gradually emerged from a state of ambiguity that typified its attitude to terrorism in the seventies. It has now realized that terrorism is a *degeneration* of the high ideal of freedom of peoples, proclaimed ever since 1917. In chapter 7 I showed how Abul Abbas 'invented' the attack on the Israeli port of Ashdod, because he knew full well that the taking of innocent hostages is contrary both to the opinion of the international community and to the policy pursued by the foremost leaders of the PLO.

However, the international community's 'response' to terrorism, and its use of the legal tools at its disposal, are not as effective as one would wish. As I indicated in chapter 1, the efficacy of those tools is substantially limited by the fact that not enough states are parties to the various international treaties relating to terrorism, as well as by the intrinsic *weakness* of these treaties. Again the *Achille Lauro* case proves my point: unlike the United States, Egypt and the Federal Republic of Germany, Italy had not yet ratified the 1979 Convention on the Taking of Hostages and was therefore not bound by the treaty's obligations. Egypt, on the other hand was bound by the 1979 Convention but failed in the event to respect it, thereby provoking the irrational response of the United States, which promptly 'hijacked' the Egyptian Boeing. In addition, Italy saw fit to disregard the provisions of its extradition treaty with the United States.

On the other hand, frustrated at the inadequacy of the legal tools at their disposal, some states decided on a dangerous course of action: they adopted a policy which increased the range of armed attacks considered legitimate. Thus, the United States and Israel have not only claimed that it is legitimate to use armed force against terrorists, jeopardizing the lives of innocent people, they have also felt they can intercept aircraft or ships of other sovereign states when they suspect there are terrorists on board. Obviously, this means responding to violence with violence. Again, the *Achille Lauro* affair confirmed some states' dangerous tendency to widen the gaps in the legal bans on the use of armed force.

Thus, the conclusion can be drawn that the *Achille Lauro* episode highlights through a prism, as it were, the weakness of the international legal regulation of state response to terrorism. The *general principles on the use of force* have been stretched and twisted by a superpower to fit its strategy and political interests. The *multilateral treaties* specially designed to allow states to cope with terrorism have gone unheeded on account of the intrinsic weakness of their enforcement mechanisms. The *bilateral treaties* aimed at better organizing close cooperation between states in various areas of crime, including terrorism, have also proved scantily effective, for they have been unable to force a contracting party to put aside short-term political or national interests for the sake of concerted action against terrorism.

In the event, one of the few positive results of the incident under consideration is the drafting of a further international treaty: the Convention for the Suppression of Unlawful Acts Against the Safety of Maritime Navigation, adopted on 10 March 1988 by a diplomatic conference convened by the International Maritime Organization (IMO).

THE *ACHILLE LAURO* AFFAIR AND PRESENT DAY TRENDS

Let me just add one last comment. It we step back and look at the *Achille Lauro* incident after a couple of years have elapsed and against the background of an international community that is continually evolving, two points emerge.

First, *individuals and groups*, who for centuries have had to suffer the actions, commands and bullying of sovereign states – those omnipotent gods – have burst upon the international scene, by hijacking a liner and undertaking other similar actions. They have moved to centre stage and forced themselves into the limelight; if only for a few days they have conditioned the behaviour of states (including one superpower) and have tried to dictate terms to them. But they came in on the wrong cue and in the wrong costume. As terrorists, they cannot expect to acquire any form of legitimacy. Terrorist actions run counter to the principles commonly accepted by the world community. Terrorists may be concerned with respect for accepted values (freedom and the self-determination of peoples), but the means they use are considered unacceptable by all, or almost all. It was only to be expected that, having played the 'lead' with sovereign states for one or two days, they should then fall under their power; having been arrested by the police, they were taken before the courts. They were thus subjected to the most conspicuous manifestations of state sovereignty. Their international 'personality' was extremely short-lived and, on the whole, counterproductive. Individuals and groups that wish to play a part on the international scene have to choose a different route from that of terrorism. This can only be achieved by a progressive transfer of powers, prerogatives and opportunities for action, to individuals and groups working *in harmony* with the establishment, and not seeking to collide with it head on. This is the only way to imbue the international community with non-governmental, and therefore more 'human', values and exigencies, without undermining the current system of sovereign states and thereby risking the loss of all the current guarantees for restraining centrifugal forces. Obviously, this will be a long and arduous task; but it is equally evident that terrorism, far from offering a solution, merely leads up a blind alley.

My second point is that, in moments of crisis like the *Achille Lauro* incident, relations between *states* that share a common political and ideological background, or are even members of the same political and military alliance, can become so strained that they may reach breaking point and allow purely national considerations to prevail. Each state ends up acting on its own. In the *Achille Lauro* case the various countries involved did try to negotiate and coordinate their action, at least at the beginning. But soon the requirements, interests and political postures of each state drifted apart, and each actor followed its own 'individualistic' bent. Thus, after a few hours, the idea of cooperation was rejected and everyone reverted to the *logic of the old international community*, or 'Cyclopean law', as Giambattista Vico called it. 'Cyclopean' in two senses: both because that law was created by giants that towered over puny individuals, crushing them beneath their will; and because the law regulated relations between ferociously egotistical Titans, 'each living in a cave with his wife and daughters, never meddling in the affairs of the others, preserving in this manner the habits of their recent origin and fiercely killing those who trespassed beyond the confines of the territory of each'.

The international community, in its new guise after World War II, is still very fragile: in times of crisis, states revert to the old individualistic patterns of behaviour typical of the period when the community was born, around the Peace of Westphalia (1648). It is a sad conclusion, but the world community with its new solidarity and cooperation is effective only, or almost only, in the everyday business of current affairs. So long as states are expected to agree on protecting their commercial, economic and social interests, and conflicts can be settled or diluted by negotiation, then all goes well. Our present-day international community is like those long-standing couples whose marriage survives in the *routine* of everyday domesticity; but should one partner develop a sudden passion for someone else, relations become fraught, turbulent, full of ill will, and, if they do not break up altogether, they limp on in semidarkness, which only a return to their humdrum daily existence can illuminate.

Documentary Sources

Within each section, documents are presented in chronological order.

Italian documents

Letter of 8 October 1985 from the Italian Ambassador to the United Nations, Maurizio Bucci, to the President of the Security Council of the United Nations, UN Doc. S/17548, 9 October 1985.

Letter of 9 October 1985 from the Italian Ambassador to the United Nations, Maurizio Bucci, to the President of the Security Council of the United Nations, UN Doc. S/17556, 9 October 1985.

Interview with G. Andreotti, in *la Repubblica*, 11 October 1985, p. 5.

Interview with Ambassador G. Migliuolo, in *la Repubblica*, 12 October 1985, p. 3.

Statement released by the Press Office of the Ministry of Foreign Affairs, in *la Repubblica*, 13–14 October 1985, p. 3.

Interview with G. Andreotti, in *Il Resto del Carlino*, 16 October 1985, p. 1.

Address made by the Prime Minister, Hon. Bettino Craxi, to the Chamber of Deputies, 17 October 1985; *Atti parlamentari*, IX legislature, debates of the session on 17 October 1985, *Resoconto stenografico* (shorthand minutes), pp. 32445–54.

Report on A. Badini's talk with Abul Abbas; Prime Minister's office, press release, 18 October 1985, p. 5.

Note from the Prime Minister's office of 22 October 1985, p. 3, published in part in *Corriere della Sera*, 23 October 1985, p. 1, under the title *Un pirata: Abbas il Capo (ma la Procura smentisce)*.

Interview with the Italian Minister of Justice, Martinazzoli, by P. Graldi, in *Corriere della Sera*, 25 October 1985, p. 2.

A. Badini, *Ecco perché, per Abbas, avevamo ragione*, in *Il Messaggero*, 19 March 1986, p. 3.

Prime Minister's office, note of 4 October 1986; published in *Corriere della Sera*, 5 October 1986. p. 2.

Court of Assize of Genoa, decision of 10 July 1986, filed with the Registrar on 27 December 1986 (typewritten text); unpublished.

Juvenile Court of Genoa, decision of 5 December 1986, filed with the Registrar on 27 December 1986 (typewritten text); unpublished.

Appellate Court of Genoa, Second Penal Section (for Juveniles), decision of 4 May 1987, filed with Registrar on 20 June 1987 (typewritten text); unpublished.

Appellate Court of Assize of Genoa, decision of 23 May 1987, filed with the Registrar on 27 July 1987 (typewritten text); unpublished.

United States documents

Statement of the State Department on 9 October 1985, in *Department of State Bulletin*, December 1985, vol. 85, p. 74.

White House statement on 9 October 1985, ibid., p. 74.

White House statement on 10 October 1985, ibid., p. 74.

President Reagan's statement to the press on 10 October 1985, in *International Legal Materials*, 1985, vol. XXIV, pp. 1512–13.

Statement of the President's first deputy spokesman to the press on 10 October 1985, ibid., pp. 1513–14.

Press conference of White House spokesman L. Speakes on 10 October 1985, published in full in the *New York Times*, 11 October 1985, p. A-12, cols 1–6.

FBI request to the Italian intelligence service (SISDE) to arrest Abul Abbas, 10 October 1985, unpublished.

Statement of Defence Secretary C. W. Weinberger on 11 October 1985, published in part in the *New York Times*, 11 October 1985, p.A-1, col. 5 and p. A-11, cols 5–6.

President Reagan's statement to the press on 11 October 1985, in *International Legal Materials*, 1985, vol. XXIV, pp. 1514–16.

Interview with Secretary of State Schultz on 11 October 1985, in *Department of State Bulletin*, December 1985, vol. 85, pp. 76–7.

Statement of National Security Advisor R. McFarlane to the press on 11 October 1985, in *International Legal Materials*, 1985, vol. XXIV, pp. 1516–24.

Warrant of arrest for Abul Abbas and others issued by the District Court Judge of the District of Columbia on 12 October 1985 (*nunc pro tunc*: 11 October 1985), ibid., pp. 1553–7.

Diplomatic note no. 1056 from the US Embassy in Rome to the Italian Ministry of Justice, requesting Abul Abbas' provisional arrest, 12 October 1985, unpublished.

Message of the US police authorities to the Italian Ministries of Interior and Justice, giving details about Abul Abbas' criminal record, of 13 October 1985, unpublished.

White House statement on 13 October 1985, in *Department of State Bulletin*, December 1985, vol. 85, pp. 77–8.

Interview with the Head of the FBI, Mr W. H. Webster, on 13 October 1985, ibid., pp. 78–9.

Interview with the Legal Adviser to the State Department, Mr A. D. Sofaer, on 13 October 1985, ibid., pp. 79–80.

Interview with Naval Secretary J. F. Lehman Jr on 13 October 1985, ibid., pp. 79–80.

Diplomatic note no. 1061 from the US Embassy in Rome to the Italian Ministry of Justice, urging the provisional arrest of Abul Abbas, 15 October 1985, unpublished.

Interview with the Head of the CIA, William Casey, in *Time*, 28 October 1985, p. 18.

Congress Joint Resolution on 6 November 1985 (Res. 228) in *International Legal Materials*, 1985, vol. XXIV, pp. 1562–4.

Aftermath of the *Achillo Lauro* incident. *Hearing and Mark up* before the Committee on Foreign Affairs and its Subcommittee on international operations, in *House of Representatives, Ninety-ninth Congress*, 1st Session on H. Con. Res. 228, 30 October, 6–7 November 1985, Washington DC, Us., Gpo. 1986.

Egyptian documents

Interview with the Egyptian Ambassador to Washington, el-Sayed Raouf el-Reedy, on ABC news on 9 October 1985, published in the *New York Times*, 10 October 1985, p. A-14, cols 3–5.

Statement of the Minister for Foreign Affairs, Esmat Abdel Meguid,

150 *Documentary Sources*

on 10 October 1985, published in part in the *New York Times*, 11 October 1985, p. A-11, cols 1–3.

Statement of President Hosni Mubarak on 10 October 1985, published in part in the *New York Times*, 11 October 1985, p. A-10, cols 5–6.

Statement of the Minister for Foreign Affairs on 11 October 1985, published in the *New York Times*, 12 October 1985, p. A-5, cols 1–3.

President Mubarak's statement to the press on 12 October 1985, published in part in the *New York Times*, 15 October 1985, p. A-10, cols 1–2.

Television interview with President Mubarak, 20 October 1985, published in part in the *New York Times*, 21 October 1985, p. A-1, col 6 and p. A-6, cols 4–6.

Interview with President Mubarak on 25 October 1985, published in part in *Time*, 28 October 1985, p. 10.

Palestinian documents

Statement on terrorism by the National Council of PLO of 22–28 November 1984, in *The Palestine Yearbook of International Law*, 1985, vol. II, p. 191.

Statement by Arafat's spokesman, Ahmed Abderrahman, on 8 October 1985, reported in part in the *New York Times*, 9 October 1985, p. A-8, col. 2.

Radio communications between the hijackers and Palestinian leaders in Port Said on 9 October 1985 (intercepted by the Israeli Intelligence), reported by F. Gerardi in *Achille Lauro – Operazione salvezza*, Milano, Rusconi, 1986, pp. 203–14.

Press conference given by Arafat on 9 October 1985, published in part in the *New York Times*, 10 October 1985, p. A-12, cols 2–6.

Statement to the press made by Arafat's collaborator, Hani el-Hassan, on 10 October 1985, summarized by the *New York Times*, 11 October 1985, p. A-11, col. 1.

Statement of the Head of the political department of PLO, Farouk Kaddoumi, on 10 October 1985, reported almost entirely in the *New York Times*, 11 October 1985, p. A-14, cols 2–4.

Statements by PLO officials in Tunis on 11 October 1985, published in part in the *New York Times*, 11 October 1985, p. A-10, cols 1–6.

Statement made by Arafat in Dakar on 12 October 1985, reported in part in the *New York Times*, 13 October 1985, p. A-21, cols 1–5.

Statement by a PLO spokesman in Tunis on 12 October 1985, published in part in the *New York Times*, 13 October 1985, p. A-21, cols 5–6.

Interview with Abul Abbas by telephone from Belgrade, 13 October 1985, published in part in the *New York Times*, 14 October 1985, p. A-11, cols 2–6.

Statements on terrorism by Arafat on 7 November 1985 in Cairo, published in *The Palestinian Yearbook of International Law*, 1985, vol. II, pp. 191–2.

Interview with Abul Abbas in *Al Qabas*, published in *L'Europeo*, 13, 1987, pp. 46–50.

Interview with Abul Abbas in *Al Majalla*, published in part in *la Repubblica*, 11 March 1987, p. 9.

United Nations documents

UN Security Council documents

S/PV.1736, 13 August 1973
S/PV.1737, 14 August 1973
S/PV.1738, 14 August 1973
S/PV.1739, 15 August 1973
S/PV.1740, 15 August 1973
S/PV.2618, 9 October 1985
S/17554, 9 October 1985
S/PV.2622, 11 October 1985
S/PV.2620, (reissued) 17 October 1985
S/PV.2651, 4 February 1986
S/PV.2655/Corr.1, 18 February 1986

UN General Assembly resolutions

31/102 of 15 December 1976
32/147 of 16 December 1977
34/145 of 17 December 1979
36/109 of 10 December 1981

38/130 of 19 December 1983
40/61 of 9 December 1985
42/159 of 7 December 1987

Bibliography

Terrorism

A. Cassese 1988: *Violence and Law in the Modern Age*. Cambridge: Polity Press.

N. Chomsky 1988: *The Culture of Terrorism*. London: Pluto Press.

Y. Dinstein 1987: The international legal response to terrorism. In *Le droit international à l'heure de sa codification. Etudes en l'honneur de R. Ago*, Milano: A. Giuffré, vol. II, pp. 139–51.

A. E. Evans and J. F. Murphy (eds) 1978: *Legal Aspects of International Terrorism*. Lexington, Mass.: Lexington Books.

W. Gutteridge (ed.) 1986: *The New Terrorism*. London: Mansell Publishing.

G. F. Intoccia 1985: International legal and policy implications of an American counterterrorist strategy. *Denver Journal of International Law and Policy*, 14, pp. 121–46.

W. Laqueur (ed.) 1987: *The Terrorism Reader: a historical anthropology*. New York: New American Library.

B. Netarryochm (ed.) 1986: *Terrorism: how the West can win*. New York: N. N. Farrar, Strauss & Giroux, Inc.

E. R. Pollock 1982/3: Terrorism as a tort in violation of the law of nations. *Fordham International Law Journal*, 6, pp. 236–60.

A. D. Sofaer 1986: Terrorism and the Law. *Foreign Affairs*, 64, pp. 901 ff.

Symposium on international terrorism 1982: *Rutgers Law Journal*, 13, pp. 453–605.

The Achille Lauro *affair*

G. R. Constantinople 1986: Towards a New Definition of Piracy:

The 'Achille Lauro' Incident. *Virginia Journal of International Law*, pp. 723–53.

E. David, November 1985: Le détournement du Boeing 737 egyptien par la chasse américaine (10–11 October 1985). *Journal des Juristes Démocrates*, p. 2.

G. De Rosa 1987: *Terrorismo forza 10*. Milano: Mondadori.

P. S. Edelman, 1 November 1985: Pirates and Passengers. *New York Law Journal*, p. 1, col. 1; p. 30.

G. Gaja 1985: Sulla repressione penale per i fatti dell' 'Achille Lauro'. *Rivista di diritto internazionale*, pp. 588–90.

F. Gerardi 1986: *Achille Lauro – Operazione salvezza*. Milano: Rusconi.

M. Halberstam 1988: Terrorism on the High Seas: The *Achille Lauro*, Piracy and the IMO Convention on Maritime Safety. *The American Journal of International Law*, pp. 269–310.

V. Lippolis 1986: Parlamento e apertura della crisi di governo: il discutibile procedente della crisi (rientrata) del governo Craxi. *Diritto e società* (new series), pp. 395–402.

A. L. Liput 1986: An Analysis of the 'Achille Lauro' Affair: Towards an Effective and Legal Method of Bringing International Terrorists to Justice. *Fordham International Law Journal*, pp. 328–72.

A. F. Lowenfeld and R. B. Glynn, 1 November 1985: Analyzing the Applicable Laws in the 'Achille Lauro' Aftermath. *New York Law Journal*, p. 1, cols 3–4, p. 3.

J. A. McCredie 1986: Contemporary Uses of Force against Terrorism: The United States Response to 'Achille Lauro' – Questions of Jurisdiction and its Exercise. *Georgia Journal of International and Comparative Law*, pp. 435–67.

G. P. McGinley 1985: The 'Achille Lauro' Affair – Implications for International Law. *Tennessee Law Review*, pp. 691–738.

J. P. Pancracio 1985: L'affaire de l''Achille Lauro' et le droit international'. *Annuaire français de droit international*, vol. 31, pp. 221–36.

J. J. Paust 1987: Extradition and United States Prosecution of the *Achille Lauro* Hostage-Takers: Navigating the Hazards. *Vanderbilt Journal of International Law*, pp. 235–57.

M. Pisani 1986: Il caso dell' 'Achille Lauro' ed il trattato di estradizione tra l'Italia e gli Stati Uniti. *Rivista di diritto internazionale privato e processuale*, pp. 775–88.

W. Richey, 7 April 1986: U.S. tries to expand array of tools to fight terrorism. *Christian Science Monitor*, p. 1, col. 1.

N. Ronzitti 1985: Alcuni problemi giuridici sollevati dal dirottamento dell' 'Achille Lauro'. *Rivista di diritto internazionale*, pp. 584–8.

N. D. Sandler, 15 October 1987: Assessing the President's action at this point may be premature (Bushwhacking the hijackers). *Los Angeles Daily Journal*, p. 4, col. 3.

H. W. Stephens 1987: Not Merely the 'Achille Lauro': the Threat of Maritime Terrorism and Piracy. *Terrorism: An International Journal*, pp. 285–96.

F. Strasser, 28 October 1985: Family may sue in hijack murder. *National Law Journal*, p. 3, col. 2.

Index

Index by Barbara Hird